Mexico

Mexico

BY DEBORAH KENT

Enchantment of the World™
Second Series

Children's Press®

An Imprint of Scholastic Inc.

NEW YORK   TORONTO   LONDON   AUCKLAND   SYDNEY
MEXICO CITY   NEW DELHI   HONG KONG
DANBURY, CONNECTICUT

A Maria Morales Luna
con mil gracias de toda la familia

Frontispiece: Caribbean Sea off Cancún

Consultant: William Beezley, PhD, Professor of History, University of Arizona

Please note: All statistics are as up-to-date as possible at the time of publication.

Book production by The Design Lab

Library of Congress Cataloging-in-Publication Data

Kent, Deborah.
  Mexico/by Deborah Kent.
     p. cm.—(Enchantment of the world, second series)
  Includes bibliographical references and index.
  ISBN-13: 978-0-531-25355-7 (lib. bdg.)
  ISBN-10: 0-531-25355-4 (lib. bdg.)
1. Mexico—Juvenile literature. 2. Mexico—History—Juvenile
literature. I. Title. II. Series.
  F1208.5.K46 2012
  972—dc22   2011010812

Mexico

Contents

Cover photo:
Young person wearing Day of the Dead mask

Mexican folk dancers

Toltec statue

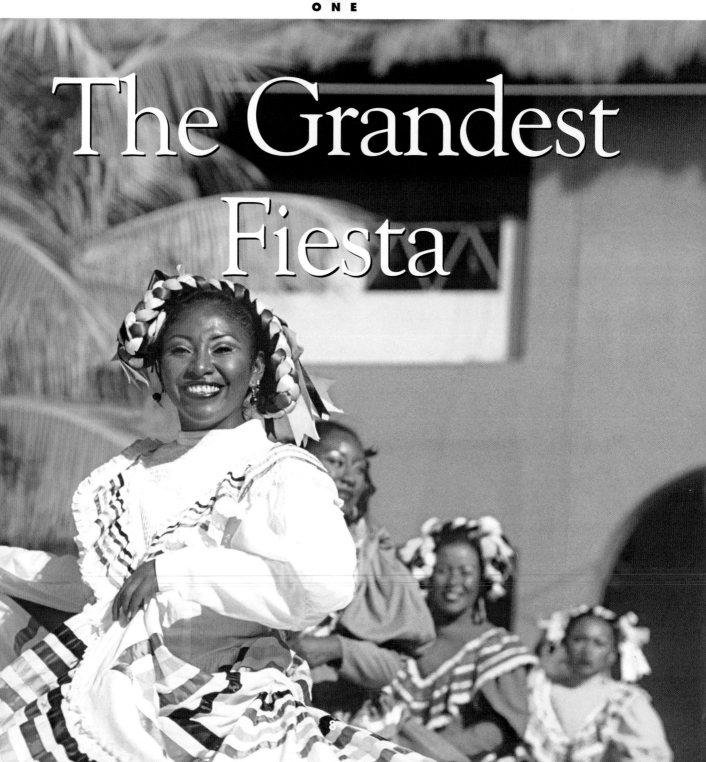

CHAPTER ONE

The Grandest Fiesta

MEXICO IS A LAND OF FIESTAS. THE MEXICAN calendar is sprinkled with saints' days and historical holidays. Each is honored with a party for the whole town. Fiestas are usually celebrated with parades featuring bands and floats. In the plaza, or town square, crowds gather to watch dancers and listen to bands play traditional mariachi music. Often, the fiesta ends with a display of pinwheels, rockets, and Roman candles glittering against the night sky.

In July 2010, Mexico launched the grandest fiesta in its long history. The Bicentennial Exposition, known as Expo 2010, marked the two hundredth anniversary of the beginning of Mexico's War of Independence. It also remembered the hundredth anniversary of the Mexican Revolution, a war that led to the system of government that exists today.

Expo 2010 was a four-month extravaganza held in the town of Silao in the state of Guanajuato, in central Mexico. The expo was celebrated with music, mime shows, and food from every region of the nation. It hosted nearly three hundred conferences and conventions, including the Festival of

Opposite: **Women often wear bright, colorful dresses when performing Mexican folk dances.**

Contemporary Art, the World Youth Conference, the Old Cars Rally, and an international chamber music festival.

An unforgettable spectacle greeted visitors on the opening day of the expo. The Floral Salute was a float covered with more than fifty thousand roses. The words "MEXICO 2010" were spelled out with braided chains of flowers. Atop the float stood the figure of Mexico's Angel of Independence, woven entirely of gold straw flowers. Hundreds of skillful hands created the Floral Salute, drawing upon traditions that reach deep into Mexico's past.

"To me the bicentennial festivities are a way for us to remember to feel proud that we are Mexicans," one visitor explained. "My children and I like to remember that our history stretches back thousands of years. The music, the murals, the sights all remind us that we belong to a nation with enormous heart."

A dancer dressed as a bouquet of flowers performs at Mexico's bicentennial celebration.

A Magnificent Land

TRAVEL BROCHURES OFTEN PAINT MEXICO AS A LAND OF sand, surf, and sunshine. With thousands of miles of coastline along the Pacific Ocean and the Gulf of Mexico, Mexico is indeed a beach lover's paradise. This picture of Mexico is far from complete, however. In fact, there is no such thing as a typical Mexican landscape. Majestic mountains, some of them capped with snow, rise in the country's interior. Dense rain forests flourish in the south. Cacti grow in dry, dusty regions. As visitors come to know Mexico better, they are entranced by its diversity.

Opposite: **Clouds hang over the mountains of southwestern Mexico.**

A Glance at the Map

On a map Mexico looks roughly like a shoe with an upturned toe. In the north the top of the shoe lies along Mexico's border with the United States. The Central American nations of Guatemala and Belize lie along the eastern edge of the shoe's toe. The tip of the toe, the Yucatán Peninsula, juts north into the Gulf of Mexico. The Pacific Ocean forms Mexico's western coastline. A long, narrow peninsula called Baja California

The Rio Grande defines part of the border between Mexico and the United States. In Mexico, the river is known as the Río Bravo del Norte.

dangles from Mexico's northwest corner like a tassel hanging down from the top of the shoe.

Mexico's border with the United States is the second longest in the world. Only the border between the United States and Canada is longer. Between Mexico and the state of Texas the border is clearly defined by a river called the Rio Grande. To the west no distinctive features mark the boundary. Instead, fences and barbed wire separate the two countries.

The border between Mexico and the United States separates nations with vastly different cultures. Mexico is a country oppressed by poverty. The United States is an economic superpower. In Mexico, a construction worker pushing a wheelbarrow might earn seven or eight dollars a day. In the United States, construction laborers are paid ten dollars an hour or more. Nowhere else on earth do such a wealthy nation and such a poor one exist as neighbors.

Looking at Mexico's Cities

The largest city in Mexico is Mexico City, the capital, which is home to more than 12 million people. Its suburb Ecatepec is the second-largest city with about 1.8 million people. The next three largest cities—Guadalajara, Puebla, and Ciudad Juárez—each have populations of around 1.5 million.

Guadalajara (right) is both an economic and a cultural center of Mexico. It is a major manufacturing city, producing textiles, electronics, food products, and more. Guadalajara's magnificently decorated cathedral draws tourists and worshippers alike. The Degollado Theater, one of the largest theaters in Latin America, is also richly decorated. Guadalajara is associated with mariachi music, and the city hosts a major mariachi festival each year.

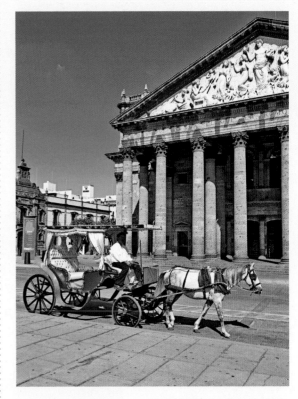

Puebla (left) sits on a high plain in the shadow of Popocatépetl and Ixtacihuatl, two major volcanoes. Earthquakes have frequently shaken Puebla, damaging some of its many historic buildings. A thousand buildings from the Spanish era still stand, however. Many are decorated with colorful tiles. These tiles are made from local clay in an elaborate time-honored process.

Ciudad Juárez, Mexico's fifth-largest city, is named after Benito Juárez, a Mexican president from the 1860s. The city is a major border-crossing point, standing across the Rio Grande from El Paso, Texas. It is home to hundreds of assembly plants. In recent years, Ciudad Juárez has experienced much violence between rival gangs that smuggle drugs into the United States.

Road Trip

A drive from Tijuana on Mexico's northern border with California to the city of Tapachula on its southeastern border with Guatemala is about 2,488 miles (4,004 km) long. The trip is just 300 miles (480 km) shorter than a drive from Los Angeles to Philadelphia in the United States.

Mexico stretches 976 miles (1,571 kilometers) north to south and is 360 miles (579 km) across at its widest point. In total, Mexico covers 758,449 square miles (1,964,374 square kilometers). Texans sometimes brag that their state is big compared to other U.S. states. This is true, but Texas would fit three times within Mexico's borders.

The Sierra Madre Occidental runs through the state of Sonora, in the northwest.

Mexico's Geographic Features

Area: 758,449 square miles (1,964,374 sq km)

Largest City: Mexico City, population 12,294,193

Highest Elevation: Pico de Orizaba, 18,410 feet (5,611 m) above sea level

Lowest Elevation: Mexicali Valley, 33 feet (10 m) below sea level

Longest River: Rio Grande, which Mexico shares with the United States, 1,248 miles (2,008 km) within Mexico

Longest River Entirely Within Mexico: Río Lerma, about 350 miles (560 km)

Largest Lake: Lake Chapala, 417 square miles (1,080 sq km)

Length of Coastlines: 5,797 miles (9,329 km)

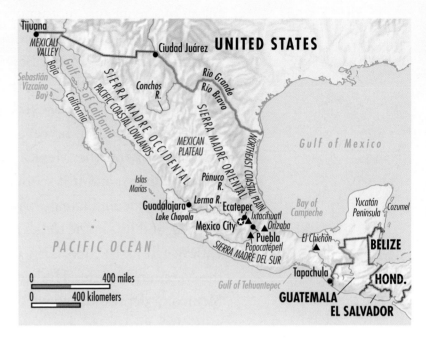

Officially Mexico is called Los Estados Unidos Mexicanos (the United Mexican States). Like its northern neighbor, Mexico is divided into states. Mexico has thirty-one states and one federal district. The federal district surrounds the nation's capital, Mexico City. Imagine a line drawn through Mexico City. Everything below that line is referred to as southern Mexico, and everything above the line is considered northern Mexico.

Running along Mexico's seacoasts are two major mountain ranges, the Sierra Madre Oriental in the east and the

Sierra Madre Occidental in the west. Roughly translated, Sierra Madre means "mother of mountains." The word *oriental* means "eastern" and the word *occidental* means "western," in both English and Spanish. Between these two mighty mountain ranges lies a broad, relatively flat region known as the Central Plateau or the Mexican Plateau. The word *flat* must be used with caution, however. Almost no land in Mexico is truly level. Even the Mexican Plateau is studded with hills and mountains, and it is scored with deep valleys.

The Mexican Plateau contains the most fertile land in Mexico, and it is home to the majority of the Mexican people. Cities such as Mexico City, Guadalajara, and Puebla lie on the Mexican Plateau. The nation's heartland is the Valley of Mexico, a depression about 60 miles (100 km) long and 40 miles (65 km) wide in the middle of the Mexican Plateau. Mexico City stands at the valley's southern tip.

The City of Eternal Spring

Cuernavaca is a lovely small city in a valley just south of Mexico City. It is often called the City of Eternal Spring. Alexander von Humboldt, a German naturalist and explorer, gave Cuernavaca its nickname in the early 1800s when he visited the city and admired its gentle climate. Cuernavaca's springlike climate is the norm throughout the year. The average temperature is 68 degrees Fahrenheit (20 degrees Celsius) year-round. But in truth this cheerful climate is not unique to Cuernavaca. Sunny skies and pleasant temperatures are common in much of the Central Plateau. Mexicans living in the region call the rare cloudy day *un día triste* (a sad day).

An Agreeable Climate

When snowstorms howl, many residents of Canada and the northern United States think of Mexico as a sun-splashed haven. These same northerners imagine that in the summer Mexico is a nightmare of heat and humidity. Because Mexico is warm during the winter, they reason, it must be absolutely sweltering in the summertime. This idea is incorrect. The Mexican Plateau, where most of the people live, enjoys a mountain climate. It is seldom sticky in the summer, and its temperatures are moderate. In fact, the Mexican Plateau is much cooler in the summer than low-lying northern cities such as Chicago, Illinois, or Toronto, Canada.

The Mexican Plateau spreads out over almost one-third of the country.

Some parts of Baja California are extremely hot and dry.

In Mexico, the most important factor in temperature is elevation. The climate does not necessarily grow warmer as one travels south, as it does in the United States. Instead, Mexico is warm along its coasts at sea level but relatively cool in the mountain regions. The Mexican coasts are called the *tierras calientes* (hot lands). Most of the plateaus are in the region called the *tierra templada* (temperate lands). The highest regions are known as the *tierras frías* (cold lands).

Mexico's climate is less than perfect, however. Many parts of the country struggle with a lack of rain. Much of northern Mexico is desert where only cacti and scrubby bushes can survive. Rainfall is more plentiful in the middle of the Mexican Plateau, where the most productive farms are found. But the Mexican Plateau can endure dismal periods of drought. Rainfall is seasonal in the highlands. The rainy season usually starts in June and extends into September. If the rain fails to fall during these months, then farmers—and the Mexican people—suffer. Rain nourishes cornfields, and the corn is made into tortillas, the common bread eaten throughout Mexico. When the rainy season fails, tortillas become scarce and the price of food soars.

During the summer and early fall, severe tropical storms sometimes lash Mexico's Gulf and Pacific coasts. These storms cause flooding, property damage, and loss of life. In October 1966, Hurricane Inez zigzagged across the Gulf and struck Mexico. Hurricane Gilbert hit the Yucatán Peninsula, roared across the Gulf, and slammed into the city of Matamoros in September 1988. Another storm, Hurricane Isidore, hit the Yucatán Peninsula in September 2002.

Hurricane Gilbert destroyed almost all of the 250 homes in Carbonera, Mexico, in 1988. To be called a hurricane, a storm must have sustained winds of at least 74 miles per hour (119 kilometers per hour).

Eruptions in 1982 created a crater 0.5 miles (1 km) across on top of El Chichón. The ash and lava destroyed about 40 square miles (100 sq km) of the surrounding rain forest.

Dangerous Grounds

On March 29, 1982, villagers in the state of Chiapas heard ominous rumblings. Plumes of smoke rose from the top of a usually peaceful mountain called El Chichón. Suddenly molten streams of lava burst from the mountain's crown and poured onto the villages below. Some two thousand people died during El Chichón's eruption.

Beneath Mexico's tranquil valleys and plateaus surge vast geological forces that can have disastrous effects. Mexico is home to some three thousand volcanoes. The most famous

A Volcano in the Making

On February 20, 1943, a farmer was driving a team of oxen in a cornfield west of Mexico City. Suddenly, he heard a strange hissing sound. He noticed a smell much like rotten eggs and saw the earth in front of him bulge and crack. From the crack rose clouds of smoke and ash. "I was so stunned I hardly knew what to do or what to think," the farmer remembered later. "I couldn't find my wife or my son or the animals." The farmer had witnessed the formation of a new volcano called Paricutín. Paricutín grew with a series of eruptions from 1943 to 1952. Today, it is a cone-shaped volcanic mountain 1,391 feet (424 m) high.

are Popocatépetl and Ixtacihuatl (Popo and Ixta), two snow-capped mountains that overlook Mexico City. Ixta is usually quiet, but Popo often sends up clouds of smoke and ash. According to legend, Popo and Ixta are man and wife. Usually they get along happily. But sometimes they quarrel, and then the ground rumbles.

Earthquakes are the scourge of the Mexican Plateau. At about seven o'clock in the morning on September 19, 1985, the ground lurched beneath Mexico City. High-rise buildings swayed in a perilous dance. Windows cracked, raining shards of jagged glass from their upper stories. Many buildings collapsed as though they were stacks of cardboard boxes. The earthquake shook the capital city for only a few seconds, but it left a terrible wake of death and destruction.

The 1985 earthquake destroyed 412 buildings in Mexico City. Another 3,100 buildings were severely damaged.

As the tremors subsided, residents sprang into action. Makeshift rescue teams found trapped survivors and pulled them from the tangled rubble. In their efforts they risked their own lives to save others. A nineteen-year-old college student explained, "There was so much dust that we had to cover our faces with handkerchiefs, and bystanders were shouting that there would be an explosion because of all the gas in the air. But the screams and cries from people buried inside the rubble were too much to bear. We just kept digging until our hands bled, without giving a thought about whether we would be blown up."

The earthquake of 1985 was the greatest natural disaster to hit Mexico in its modern history. The government announced that ten thousand people died because of the tremor. Many experts believe the true death toll was twice as high. About one hundred thousand people were left homeless.

The Mexican Plateau is more prone to earthquakes than the U.S. state of California. Certainly another deadly earthquake will strike again, but no one can predict when it will happen. Mexicans shrug their shoulders and say, *¿Quién sabe?* (Who knows?) They believe they will pull through the next natural disaster as they always have in the past.

Earthquakes often rock Mexico City. Here, office workers wait outside following a quake in 2009.

From Deserts to Rain Forests

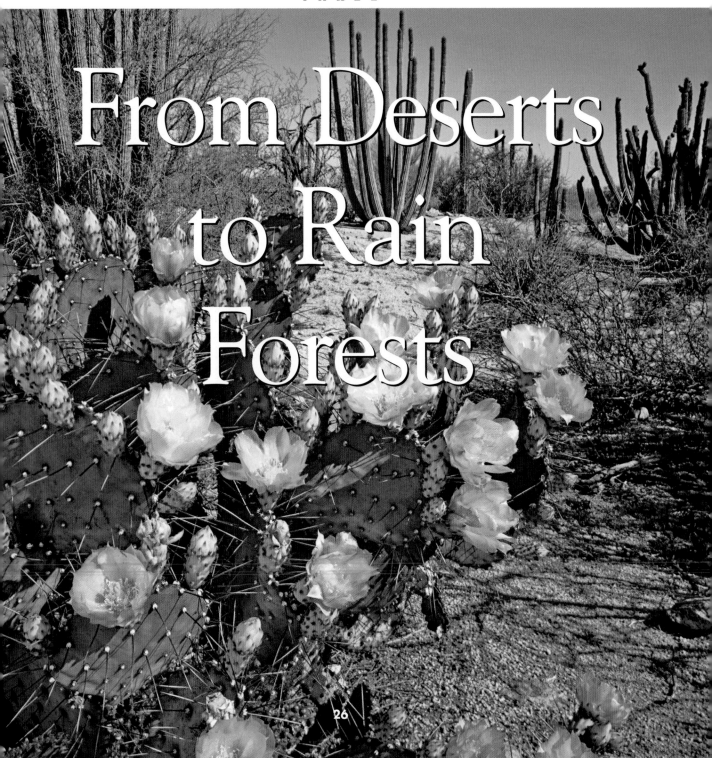

W HEN A FOREIGNER BECOMES FLUENT IN SPANISH AND comfortable with local customs, Mexicans say fondly, "¡*Es más mejicana que los nopalitos!*" ("He or she is more Mexican than the nopal cactus!") Several species of nopal, or prickly pear, are common in Mexico, and some are raised for their juicy fruit. The hardy nopal, which manages to flourish even in the desert, has become a symbol of the Mexican people and appears on the national flag.

In Mexico the fruit of the nopal is called the *tuna*. It is covered with fine, hairlike spines. The spines will embed themselves into the hand of anyone foolish enough to grab the fruit, and it may take days to remove them all. It takes care and skill to peel the tuna with a sharp knife and make it safe for eating. Still, the delicious fruit is well worth the trouble. The lobes of the nopal cactus are also edible. Mexicans eat nopal with eggs, with beans, and in many other dishes. In the 1990s scientists discovered that the nopal is rich in vitamins. It has many health benefits and may be helpful to people who have the disease diabetes.

Opposite: **There are more than two hundred species of prickly pear. All are native to the Western Hemisphere.**

Hardy plants such as the Spanish dagger yucca, which has long, sharp, stiff fronds, thrive in the deserts of Mexico.

The nopal grows throughout much of Mexico, but many other plants live only in certain areas. The deserts, rain forests, and coastal regions each have their own plant and animal communities.

The Desert Landscape

Mexico is home to the greatest number of types of cacti in the world. The organ pipe cactus, which grows in the northern part of the country, has groups of thick stems that rise from the ground, looking somewhat like the pipes of a church organ. The organ pipe cactus grows very slowly and may live up to 150 years.

Only the hardiest trees grow in the desert. The mesquite is a small tree with needle-sharp thorns. It manages to survive in dry regions because it sends its long roots deep into the ground in search of water. The roots have been known to reach a length of 197 feet (60 meters). The mesquite produces seedpods that are sometimes ground to make flour. Mesquite wood burns slowly and is often used in grilling. The aromatic smoke gives food a unique flavor.

In Mexico's mountainous areas rainfall is usually limited to the summer months. During most of the year the plant life in the mountains looks much like that of the lower deserts. When the rainy season begins, however, the mountains and high plateaus turn green and flowers burst into bloom. Even the cacti bear glorious blossoms.

Many kinds of reptiles live in Mexico's deserts. These include rattlesnakes and several species of lizards. The Gila

Corn, Mexico's Staple

Corn is the most important food plant raised in Mexico. Corn flour, or masa, is the basis for the tortilla, the flat bread that is eaten with nearly every meal. The ancestor of today's corn plant is a wild grass called teosinte that grows in central Mexico. Humans began to raise teosinte about seven thousand years ago. Gradually it evolved into the various corn plants that we know today. Corn became such an important food source that the Mexican peoples believed it had been given to them by the gods. From Mexico corn spread north and south. It became a staple food for most of the indigenous peoples of the Americas.

Hunters to the Rescue

The rare Bolson tortoise lives only in a desert area of the state of Sonora. When it is fully grown, its shell may be 18 inches (46 centimeters) across. Until recently, the Bolson tortoise was hunted for food. So many were killed that it was on the verge of extinction. The Mexican government established a reserve to protect the tortoises. Former tortoise hunters now gather eggs to be hatched in the reserve's laboratory. The young tortoises are raised in captivity and released in the wild when they are big enough to avoid being eaten by coyotes and other predators.

monster and the Mexican beaded lizard, both found in Mexico's deserts, are the only poisonous lizards on earth.

Hawks and vultures circle above the desert landscape in search of food. In the evening, coyotes' calls echo across the land, but humans seldom see the wily creatures. The antelope jackrabbit of Sonora and Chihuahua makes spectacular bounds on its long, muscular hind legs.

A Living Tank

Much like a military tank, the nine-banded armadillo is covered with plates of armor to protect it from its enemies. It is found throughout Mexico, from the deserts of the north to the tropical rain forests of the south. Armadillos live in burrows and eat ants, termites, and other insects. In recent years, armadillos have been expanding their range into the United States. They have been found as far north as southern Illinois.

Mexico's rain forest is the northernmost segment of a band of rain forest that stretches through Central America and into South America's Amazon River basin. With rainfall throughout the year, the rain forest nurtures a rich array of plants and animals. Spider monkeys swing from the treetops, and howler

The spider monkey has a long, flexible tail that it uses almost like a hand. The monkey uses the tail to balance as it walks and can grab a branch by wrapping its tail around it.

From Pygmy Mice to Whales

Mexico is home to 502 species of mammals. Only Indonesia has more mammal species, with a grand total of 539. Mexico's mammals range from right and humpback whales that cruise the offshore waters to tiny shrews, moles, and pygmy mice, creatures so small that they go largely unnoticed by humans.

monkeys give shrill, barking cries. Hundreds of bird species from the United States and Canada spend the winter months in the forests of Veracruz, Chiapas, and Yucatán.

Altogether southern Mexico has more than 160 million acres (64 million hectares) of forest, covering about 33 percent of the nation's land. The forests are rapidly disappearing, however. Thousands of acres of trees are cut down each year to make way for farmland, roads, and towns. Mexico lost more than 12 million acres (nearly 5 million ha) of forest between 1990 and 2005.

The Mexican government has taken major steps to preserve the country's rain forests. It has established a series of natural protected areas in the southern part of the country

The Poinsettia: A Christmas Favorite

During the holiday season families in the United States and Canada often add a potted poinsettia to their festive decorations. The poinsettia grows wild in Mexico's rain forests, where it can reach a height of 12 feet (3.6 m). In 1828, the U.S. minister to Mexico, Joel Robert Poinsett, saw the plant and was delighted by its red flowers and leaves. He shipped several plants to friends in the United States. The plant immediately became popular, and by 1836 it was known as the poinsettia after the man who made it famous.

Mexico's National Bird

The national bird of Mexico is the crested caracara, a large bird of prey found in deserts and coastal areas. It has a black crest, an orange-red beak, and long yellow legs. The caracara was sacred to some of Mexico's native peoples, and its image has been found in ancient drawings.

as reserves and national parks. Today about 15 percent of the land in southern Mexico is under government protection.

The rain forest is home to an astounding variety of creatures. Baird's tapir ranges south from the states of Veracruz and Oaxaca. Weighing up to 660 pounds (300 kilograms), the tapir has a long, trunklike nose. It moves slowly on land, but it

Experts estimate that fewer than 5,000 Baird's tapirs remain in the wild. Fewer than 1,500 of those live in Mexico.

The silky anteater is the smallest of all anteaters. It grows only 14 to 17 inches (36 to 43 cm) long.

is a fast swimmer. The northern tamandua is a relative of the anteater. Its claws and tail help it climb trees.

Scientists still have a great deal to learn about the animals of the rain forest. Many of these creatures live in the canopy of interlocking branches high above the ground, and scientists have few opportunities to observe them. One of these mysterious creatures is the silky anteater, which spends most of its life in the treetops. It has soft golden-brown fur and two long curving claws on each of its front feet.

Wild Cats of Mexico

Several members of the cat family live in Mexico. The cougar, or puma, hunts among Mexico's mountains and canyons. Although the cougar sometimes kills livestock, it usually eats deer and smaller animals such as rabbits. The ocelot is a much smaller cat that was once hunted for its beautiful fur. Now that it is protected, the ocelot is making a healthy comeback. The mighty jaguar (right) is the largest cat in the Americas and the third largest on earth. Only the lion and tiger are bigger. Jaguars prefer the rain forest, although they are sometimes also found in northern Mexico. Unlike most members of the cat family, the jaguar is a good swimmer.

Watch Where You Step!

Swimmers at Mexico's beaches must be careful not to come in contact with stinging jellyfish. The tentacles of most jellyfish species can give painful stings, and the stings of a few species are poisonous. On land, too, Mexico has a few creatures that can be poisonous to humans. Of Mexico's more than two thousand spider species, the black widow, brown widow, and brown recluse can be deadly. Scorpions are common in Mexico, but only a few kinds have a dangerous sting. Mexico has poisonous coral snakes and several rattlesnake species. Most of the country's poisonous creatures are shy and try to stay away from humans. People are rarely bitten or stung.

Along the Shore

The waters off Mexico's long Gulf and Pacific coasts are alive with fish, shellfish, and aquatic mammals. The Caribbean manatee lives in the tropical rivers and bays of eastern Mexico. Schools, or pods, of bottlenose dolphins play around fishing boats and cruise ships. Several species of whales can be seen off Mexico's coasts as well.

Among the fish that swim in Mexican waters are sharks, stingrays, flounders, sole, and flying fish. Shrimps, crabs, and mussels thrive in the coastal shallows.

Tragedies and Triumphs

SCHOLARS BELIEVE THAT PEOPLE FIRST ENTERED THE North American continent by crossing over the Bering Strait from Asia thousands of years ago. Ten to fifteen thousand years ago people reached the land now called Mexico.

The first Mexicans were hunters who stalked deer, elk, and other game. Among the animals they hunted were mastodons and mammoths—large elephant-like creatures—that once roamed the land. In addition to game, the early people ate wild roots, fruits, and nuts.

Opposite: **The Maya built El Castillo pyramid at Chichén Itzá between the ninth and twelfth centuries CE.**

In the Beginning

The creation stories of native peoples provide different explanations for how people first arrived in North America. Some stories say that gods brought the indigenous peoples into being on the soil of the Americas. According to the Maya, all Maya are descended from an ear of corn that the corn god (shown left) transformed in order to populate the planet.

Corn was important to all native groups in Mexico. This painting shows Aztec women making cornmeal tortillas.

About seven thousand years ago, people in Mexico made a revolutionary discovery. They learned to plant corn. Using sticks, they made holes in the ground into which they dropped corn kernels. At some point the ancient cooks developed corn tortillas and corn cakes (tamales). Experts believe that corn was first grown near the Mexican city of Puebla.

Long-Arm Throw

Mexican hunters used a spear-throwing device called the atlatl. The atlatl was a forked stick that helped the hunter throw a spear long distances with great force.

Tests show that a hunter armed with an atlatl can throw a spear the length of a football field. Some Mexican hunters used atlatls to spear fish.

With corn as their staple food, men and women settled in farming villages. Eventually these villages grew into advanced agricultural societies.

The first advanced farming culture was that of the Olmecs, who lived in the Gulf of Mexico region. The Olmecs are famous for stone carvings of colossal heads. Some of these heads weigh 40 tons (36 metric tons), as much as a heavy tank from World War II. Seventeen heads have been dug up and, curiously, many of them have African facial features. People also see Asian features in the carvings. Could there have been contact between the Olmecs and people from Africa or Asia? Scientists say no, but history is full of mysteries. Such contact cannot be ruled out completely.

Each colossal Olmec head is different from the others. Some people have suggested they might be portraits of rulers.

In Guatemala and southern Mexico lived a brilliant people called the Maya. The Maya built cities graced with tall pyramids. Maya society reached its peak between 200 and 800 CE. The Maya were scientists, astronomers, and mathematicians. They seemed obsessed with the passage of time. Maya scholars created amazingly accurate calendars, some of which measured time more than five thousand years into the future. No one knows why they needed calendars that projected time so far ahead. Their "long-count" calendar abruptly ends with December 21, 2012. Some doomsayers claim the world will end on that date.

In ancient times as well as today, the Valley of Mexico was the region's heartland. In about 200 BCE a great city was built in the valley, made up of pyramids and temples. Centuries later a people called the Aztecs came upon this wondrous city. They believed ordinary human beings could not have built it. It could only be the creation of gods. The Aztecs named the ancient city Teotihuacán, "Place of the Gods."

Teotihuacán Today

Today, Teotihuacán is a major archaeological site and a popular tourist attraction. At its height, some two hundred thousand people lived in the city. Teotihuacán was abandoned in 700 CE. Why the people left the city is unknown. It appears that their departure was sudden. The end of Teotihuacán is yet another unsolved historical mystery.

The Toltec culture rose in the Valley of Mexico between 800 and 1000 CE. The Toltecs were builders, warriors, and poets. They dominated the valley until the arrival of a powerful new culture group, the Aztecs.

A legend says that the Aztecs once lived in a marvelous land called Aztlán. It was a paradise of flowing rivers and lakes alive with fish. Somehow the people angered a powerful god. The legend does not explain how they offended the deity. The god drove the Aztecs from their earthly paradise, and they became wanderers in the desert. Another god told them to search for a place where they would see an eagle perched on a cactus, eating a snake. On that spot they should build a city. In the year 1325, the Aztecs saw the miraculous vision.

Many Toltec sites include statues of a man reclining with his head turned to the side. Experts believe Toltecs placed bowls filled with offerings to the gods on the statues' stomachs.

This drawing depicts an eagle landing on a cactus, showing the Aztec people where to build their city.

The cactus was on an island in Lake Texcoco. The Aztecs built a city on the island and named it Tenochtitlán, "Place of the Cactus."

The Aztecs were aggressive warriors and tireless builders. They founded an empire in central Mexico that eventually stretched from the Gulf of Mexico to the Pacific Ocean. Tenochtitlán, today's Mexico City, served as the Aztec capital. It was a gleaming city in the middle of the lake. Mighty pyramids rose beside canals and ruler-straight streets. Beholding this magnificent city an Aztec poet wrote:

> The city is spread out in circles of jade
> Radiating flashes of light . . .
> Beside it the lords are borne in boats:
> Over them extends a flowery mist.

Religion dominated Aztec thought. The people credited their gods with their remarkable success. It was, after all, the gods who guided their progress from a wandering desert tribe to the greatest power in Mexico. To keep their gods happy, the Aztecs offered sacrifices in the form of human hearts. In the sacrificial ceremony, an Aztec priest or official held the victim down on a stone altar. A priest cut open the victim's chest, reached into the cavity, seized the heart, and held it up, still beating, to the sun or to a statue of a god.

Every ancient Mexican culture, even the Maya, conducted bloody sacrificial rituals. But the Aztecs carried human sacrifice to the greatest extremes. According to their own records, Aztec priests regularly sacrificed thousands of people at a time.

This painting by Diego Rivera, one of the greatest Mexican artists of the twentieth century, depicts a bustling market day in the Aztec capital.

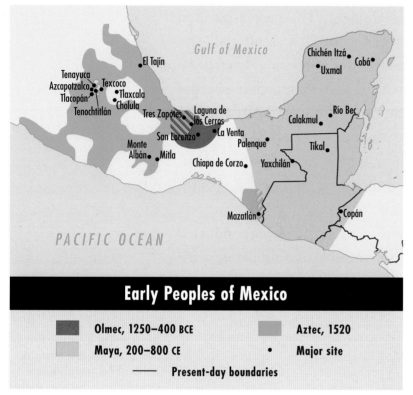

Early Peoples of Mexico

■	Olmec, 1250–400 BCE	■	Aztec, 1520
■	Maya, 200–800 CE	•	Major site
	— Present-day boundaries		

In 1502, the nobleman Montezuma became the emperor of the Aztecs. He believed that he was the most powerful man on earth. Yet Montezuma was troubled. A comet with three heads hung over the evening sky for weeks. Residents of Tenochtitlán claimed they heard a woman weeping at night, crying over the deaths of her sons. Montezuma worried that these strange signs were omens of dire events to come.

Montezuma was himself a priest. All his life he had studied the legend of a god named Quetzalcoatl. The legend promised that some day Quetzalcoatl would land on the Gulf Coast, march over the mountains, and claim the Aztec Empire as his own. In 1519, Montezuma heard reports that large boats with clouds flying above them had appeared on the Gulf Coast. In ancient pictures Quetzalcoatl was drawn as a white man with a beard. The reports said the captain of this mysterious fleet was a bearded white man. It is little wonder that Montezuma was troubled. He believed he would soon have to confront a god.

For almost thirty years Spanish adventurers had occupied settlements on islands in the Caribbean Sea. They hoped to expand the Spanish Empire, but mostly they sought gold to build their personal fortunes. In 1519, the Spanish adventurer Hernán Cortés sailed west from Cuba with an army of about four hundred men. On the coast of Mexico he fought with the indigenous peoples, but he quickly made peace. Wherever he went, he asked where he could find gold. Time and again the people pointed to the mountains and said, "México, México." Mexico was the coastal people's name for the great city of Tenochtitlán.

Grimly Montezuma waited for the arrival of Cortés and his army. Stories spread regarding the otherworldly might of the foreigners. They fought with sticks that spurted fire, roared like thunder, and killed from a distance. Surely their leader must be Quetzalcoatl, the returning god. When Montezuma finally met Cortés in November of 1519, he welcomed the Spaniard as a god.

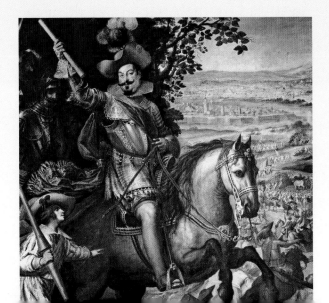

Miraculous Beasts

The Spanish army brought about a dozen horses to Mexico. The people of Mexico had never seen such wondrous animals. At first they believed that horse and rider were a single creature. The coastal people were astonished when they saw a Spaniard fall from his horse and quickly remount. Some concluded that the amazing beast could break itself apart and put itself back together at will.

The Spaniards killed Montezuma in 1520 and destroyed Tenochtitlán the following year.

For almost six months the Spaniards lived as guests of the Aztecs. But their welcome wore thin. Although they were given fine foods, rich garments, and beautiful jewelry, the Spaniards were never satisfied. They demanded gold constantly. As the weeks passed, the Aztecs realized that the foreigners were not gods as they had believed at first. They were ordinary men, and most of them were driven by greed.

Early in 1520, war flared between the Aztecs and the Spaniards. Cortés was a determined military commander. He organized rival tribes, who also hated the Aztecs, to help him in his conquest. After months of fighting, Cortés and his army finally triumphed. The Aztec Empire was crushed, and the great city of Tenochtitlán was destroyed.

Mexico, now called New Spain, became a prized colony in Spain's vast empire. The conquerors introduced the Spanish language and the Roman Catholic faith to Mexico's indigenous peoples. Mexico was not rich in gold, but the Spaniards discovered highly profitable veins of silver. Colonial Mexico became the world leader in silver production.

Mexican towns were built in the traditional Spanish style. Each town had a central plaza

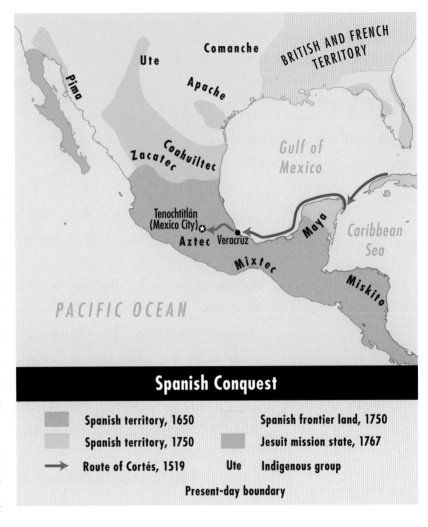

Spanish Conquest

	Spanish territory, 1650		Spanish frontier land, 1750
	Spanish territory, 1750		Jesuit mission state, 1767
→	Route of Cortés, 1519	Ute	Indigenous group
	Present-day boundary		

flanked by a church and a government building. Mexico City was built on the ruins of Tenochtitlán to serve as the capital of New Spain. Exploring expeditions fanned north and south to see what riches the new land possessed. Explorers under Francisco Vásquez de Coronado became the first Europeans to see the magnificent Grand Canyon of Arizona.

The Deadly Import

The Spaniards brought a deadly weapon with them to New Spain in the form of disease-causing microbes. Diseases such as smallpox, diphtheria, and measles were unknown in the Americas. These diseases had been with Europeans for hundreds of years, and the Spaniards' bodies had learned to fight them off. Native Mexicans had never before encountered these diseases so they had no such protection. They died in horrifying numbers. When the first Spaniards arrived, as many as twenty-five million people lived in Mexico. After one hundred years the population had dropped to little more than one million.

For three hundred years Mexico remained a Spanish colony. Under Spanish rule, the Mexicans were treated as a conquered people. Mexico had three social groups: whites, or people of pure European descent; people of mixed race, or mestizos; and Africans, who had been brought to New Spain to work as slaves. Indians were treated as a separate category entirely. The whites held the wealth and political power. Mestizos received minor privileges, and most Africans were enslaved. Indians were seen as barely human and were denied the most basic rights. There were also divisions within the classes. Whites born in Spain mistrusted those who were born in New Spain. Officials of the powerful Catholic Church clashed with officials of the government.

Townspeople line the streets as the leader of New Spain passes by.

Father Miguel Hidalgo (in black) leads the Mexican revolt. Painting by Juan O'Gorman.

Independence

In the early 1800s, a forbidden word, *independencia* (independence), was whispered in New Spain. Those people seeking freedom from Spanish rule had to keep their activities and even their conversations a secret. Any plot against Spanish rule was punishable by death.

Despite the dangers, an independence movement sprang up in the Mexican state of Guanajuato. Father Miguel Hidalgo, a priest from the village of Dolores (today called Dolores Hidalgo), led the movement. According to legend, Father Hidalgo rang a bell to summon the villagers on the evening of September 16, 1810. When the people gathered in the church, he gave a rousing speech, calling for independence from Spain.

With Father Hidalgo in charge, a ragtag army of peasants marched into the city of Guanajuato, the state capital. A terrible battle broke out. The rebels triumphed, but the blood and death of battle left the gentle priest shaken. Father Hidalgo lacked the resolve to lead his army to its next logical goal: the conquest of Mexico City. Without a leader, the peasant soldiers wandered home. Father Hidalgo was arrested and put to death.

After Father Hidalgo's death, another priest, José María Morelos, took up the cause of independence. Overseas, a host of revolutions rocked Europe. French leader Napoléon Bonaparte tried to establish his empire across Europe, and he

Hero or Criminal?

During the Battle of Guanajuato, men and women loyal to Spain took shelter in a thick-walled granary called the Alhóndiga. After a long siege, the revolutionary army broke into the Alhóndiga and slaughtered the people inside. Spanish authorities later used the building to punish the rebel leaders. Father Hidalgo and three other revolutionaries were beheaded. Spanish officials placed their heads in cagelike boxes and hung them from the corners of the granary. The Alhóndiga still stands in the center of Guanajuato. The names of the four revolutionaries—Father Miguel Hidalgo (right), General Ignacio Allende, and the soldiers Juan Aldama and Mariano Jiménez—are carved on the corners near the roof. The four men were condemned as criminals by the Spaniards, but they are honored as heroes in Mexican history.

Mexicans celebrate their independence in 1821 by greeting the new Mexican leader, Agustín de Iturbide.

replaced Spain's king with his brother. Although Napoléon's defeat allowed Spain's King Ferdinand VII to return to the throne, he could not halt the movement for independence. Mexico achieved its freedom in 1821. An independent Mexico was born.

The Early Independence Years

Independence did not usher in freedom and prosperity, as Hidalgo and other leaders had hoped. Sadly, Mexico fell under the control of a series of brutal dictators. The class system remained firmly in place. The rich lived in splendor like royalty, while masses of poor people struggled to feed their families. Furthermore, tensions mounted between Mexico and its neighbor, the United States.

Santa Anna

The most prominent dictator in the years after independence was Antonio López de Santa Anna. Born into a wealthy family, Santa Anna served eleven terms as Mexico's president. Time after time he was overthrown and driven out of office, and out of the country, but he always managed to return to power. Santa Anna was Mexico's leading army general.

When Mexico became independent it possessed an enormous territory. It extended north of the Rio Grande and included the U.S. states of Texas, Arizona, New Mexico, and California, as well as parts of Nevada and Utah. This vast region north of the Rio Grande was called the Northern Frontier. Few Mexican settlers lived there. The empty lands drew the attention of the ever-expanding United States.

Then trouble began in Texas. For years the Mexican government had allowed American pioneers to establish farms in

Slavery and the Texans

U.S. history books often say that the Texas rebels fought for freedom. Nevertheless, many of them were slaveholders who came from southern states. Slavery was illegal in Mexico. The Texans resented Mexico's opposition to slavery. Ironically, one of the "freedoms" they fought for was the right to own slaves.

the Texas region. The Texas pioneers were required to become Mexican citizens and to obey laws issued by Mexican officials. In the 1830s, the Texans rebelled against Mexican authority. They formed their own country. Mexican general Antonio López de Santa Anna led an army against the rebels. In the spring of 1836, Santa Anna crushed the upstart Texans in the Battle of the Alamo. About 180 Texans were killed, including the U.S. frontier heroes Davy Crockett and James Bowie.

The struggles in Texas set the stage for a wider war between Mexico and the United States. The U.S.-Mexican War was fought from 1846 to 1848. The Mexicans fought bravely, but they suffered from outdated weapons and a lack of supplies. During the two-year conflict, Mexico failed to win a single battle. As a result of the war, the United States acquired all

U.S troops attack Mexico City in 1847. At the end of the U.S.-Mexican War, Mexico was forced to give the United States all of California, Nevada, and Utah and parts of New Mexico, Arizona, Wyoming, and Colorado.

of Mexico's Northern Frontier. The loss of California was especially hard to take. Gold was discovered in California in 1848, and the once sleepy province became a wealthy region almost overnight.

More wars followed the conflict with the United States. In the late 1850s Mexicans fought a bloody civil war called the War of the Reform. The conflict pitted the liberals (those who wished to separate the church and state, and make other changes—or reform—to the government) against the conservatives, who resisted change. The Catholic Church backed the conservatives, giving the War of the Reform a passionate religious element. The French emperor Napoléon III saw an opportunity to send an army to invade Mexico in 1862 in order to install a European emperor, Maximilian I. The French hoped to develop Mexico as a colony. Benito Juárez led the Mexican people in the fight against the French, and Maximilian I was executed in 1867.

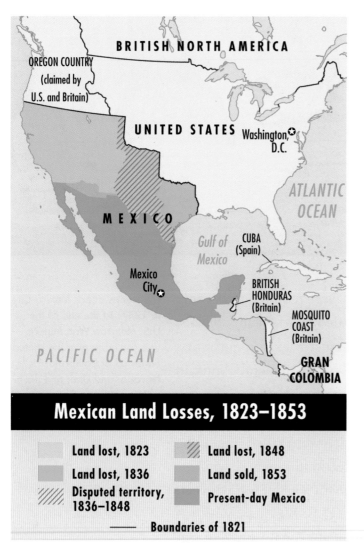

Mexican Land Losses, 1823–1853

- Land lost, 1823
- Land lost, 1836
- Disputed territory, 1836–1848
- Land lost, 1848
- Land sold, 1853
- Present-day Mexico
- —— Boundaries of 1821

Benito Juárez

Through the turmoil of the War of the Reform and the French Intervention, one leader, Benito Juárez, inspired the people. Juárez became president in 1858. He was a Zapotec Indian, the first Indian ever to serve as president of Mexico. Juárez believed that Mexico had to adopt the rule of law in order to end the almost constant revolutions and civil wars. Today he is hailed as the savior of the Mexican republic.

Revolution!

One hero in the war against the French occupation was Porfirio Díaz. Building on his status as a war hero, Díaz took office as president in 1877. Except for one brief term, he remained the nation's leader for more than thirty years.

Díaz was a dictator who dealt harshly with dissenting politicians. He offered rivals a choice: *pan o palo* (bread or the club). This policy meant that those who worked with him were rewarded (given bread), and those who worked against him were beaten down (given the club). Díaz's rule put an end to military revolts and civil wars. Mexico's economy improved as 9,000 miles (14,500 km) of railroad tracks were laid down and steel plants opened in the north.

Díaz was determined to transform Mexico into a modern country. His budget included little money for public education. By 1900, only 15 percent of the Mexican people could read or sign their names. The ownership of land remained a burning issue, dividing the rich from the poor. Under Díaz

A band of Francisco Madero's followers ride into a Mexican town in 1911.

only 2 percent of Mexican farmers owned their own land. Masses of people worked as hired hands on vast haciendas owned by the wealthy few.

In 1910, Mexicans rallied behind a mild-mannered land-owner, Francisco Madero. At first Díaz reacted in his usual manner—he had Madero thrown in jail. But a revolt had begun. Díaz was forced to flee the country. Madero was elected president in an open and honest election.

Almost immediately, army generals plotted against the new president. Madero's election sparked a new civil war, a revolution. Madero was assassinated in 1913.

The Mexican Revolution was a bloody conflict that pitted the rich against the poor. More than one million people died in the fighting or from the famine and disease caused by warfare. About one in seven Mexicans died or fled the country. Heroes rose and faded from the scene. Pancho Villa was a cattle thief who became a revolutionary hero. Villa led armies in the north. Emiliano Zapata organized the peasants of southern Mexico into a dreaded fighting force. Cleverest of all the generals was Álvaro Obregón, who studied history and used the tactics of military science.

The Mexican Revolution continued until 1940, although the violence was not as widespread after 1920. Obregón became president in 1920 and brought some order to the war-torn country. The revolution laid the foundation for the modern Mexican republic. After 1920, the country started major programs in support of land reform, labor unions, primary education, and public health.

The Zapata Legacy

In the hearts of many Mexicans, Emiliano Zapata shone as the revolution's brightest star. He was a mestizo farmer who rallied peasants with the battle cry "Land and Liberty!" In 1919, Zapata was gunned down by rivals, but his spirit never died. According to legend, Zapata still rides at night through the mountains of southern Mexico.

José Vasconcelos, Mexico's Educator

José Vasconcelos is regarded as the most important education leader in Mexican history. As secretary of education under President Álvaro Obregón (1921–1924), he created new schools in rural areas throughout the country. Vasconcelos believed that people from the humblest backgrounds had the ability to grasp complex ideas. In his book *The Cosmic Race* (1925), he suggested that the earth's races should blend and become one. He believed the mestizos were the Cosmic race.

Modern Mexico

Not everyone accepted the revolutionary programs. A rebellion called the Cristero War broke out in 1927. This three-year conflict was led by Roman Catholics who believed that the new government of Mexico opposed the Church. In 1928, Obregón, who had just won a second term as president, sat in a Mexico City restaurant. A young artist approached him and asked to sketch his picture. Obregón agreed to pose. Suddenly the artist pulled a pistol from his pocket and shot and killed the president. The artist was a Catholic who believed it was his God-given duty to assassinate Obregón.

A new president, Lázaro Cárdenas, was elected in 1934. Cárdenas was devoted to improving the lives of the poor. As president he broke up large estates and distributed land to landless farmers. In 1938, Cárdenas nationalized Mexico's oil fields. He took profitable oil wells from U.S. and British owners and placed them under Mexican control. This act endeared him to Mexicans who believed foreigners had too much power over their nation's economy.

Mexico played an important role on the side of the Allies in World War II. The Allies, the countries fighting Germany and Japan, included the United States, Great Britain, and Russia. Mexico provided oil, lead, silver, mahogany, and many other raw materials to the war effort. Mexicans also provided a major workforce in the United States to help replace men who were fighting. These Mexican guest workers were called *braceros*. Many Mexicans also joined the U.S. military. They fought together as Air Force Squadron 201.

A *bracero* picks carrots on an American farm. The Bracero Program lasted until 1964.

Acapulco became a popular resort town in the 1950s. Hotels were built lining the beach.

After World War II, Mexico became a popular destination for American, Canadian, and European tourists. Acapulco, famed for its silvery beaches, drew millions of vacationers. Hundreds of hotels opened in Acapulco and other resort cities. Tourism became the nation's leading source of jobs.

Mexico was selected to host the 1968 Olympic Games, an event certain to draw many thousands of visitors. Tourist brochures portrayed Mexico as a peaceful land of happy, contented people. This image was wildly misleading. Poor families lived in dismal huts in the shadow of the glass and steel hotels. Railroad workers and even doctors went on strike to improve their lives. Every year a million or more young people entered the job market, but many could not find work. Ten days before the opening of the Olympic Games, frustration boiled over. Police confronted a noisy crowd of protesters at a Mexico City plaza called Tlatelolco. Suddenly the plaza exploded with gunfire and screams. Later the government announced that forty-nine people had been killed in the melee. Independent observers claimed that there were between three hundred and five hundred victims, and that the army fired on unarmed students. Nevertheless, the Olympic Games of 1968 were held as planned. Visitors from all over the world enjoyed the traditional Mexican delights—food, music, and friendly people.

The U.S. team marches into Olympic Stadium during the opening ceremony of the 1968 Olympic Games in Mexico City.

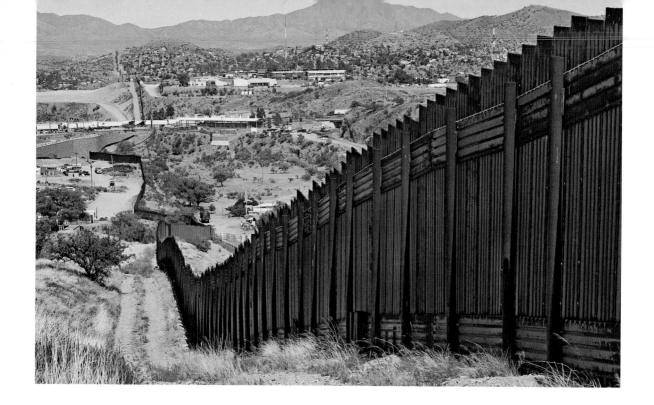

A high fence separates the cities of Nogales, Mexico, and Nogales, Arizona.

The Mexican economy failed to improve in the late 1900s and early 2000s. Many Mexican workers decided that their only chance to survive was to go to El Norte, the north, meaning the United States. For a poor Mexican the decision was a matter of simple arithmetic. A factory worker in the United States earned six dollars or more an hour. The same factory work in Mexico paid less than six dollars a day. Thousands of workers crossed the border seeking jobs. Many crossed illegally, without proper papers. U.S. officials built strong fences and hired extra police to patrol the border. Yet the workers, desperately seeking a living wage, continued to migrate to El Norte. Some workers attempted to make the crossing time after time until they finally managed to slip past the patrols.

In recent years a brutal drug war has wracked northern Mexico. Gangs of drug dealers battle the police and fight with

Border Crossing

Liliana Zúñiga grew up in the Mexican state of Guanajuato. After struggling to earn a living in Mexico, she decided to leave for El Norte. She knew that she could not get the documents necessary to immigrate legally. Her sister helped her gather enough money to hire a "coyote," a person who illegally transports Mexicans across the border. The coyote gave her a set of forged documents. He also gave her a false name and a story about her background. Heading north in the coyote's car, Liliana practiced her story over and over. The drive was long, and she fell asleep in the backseat. When she awoke she was in Texas. The border patrols never even questioned her. Liliana found a job in a coffee shop in Dallas. Eventually she married a U.S. citizen and obtained documents that allow her to live legally in the United States.

one another. The gangs are in the business of smuggling drugs such as cocaine and marijuana into the United States. People in the United States are the world's greatest consumers of illegal drugs, and drug gangs buy almost all of their guns in

Mexicans try to make it across the rushing Tijuana River and into the United States. An estimated seven hundred thousand Mexicans sneak into the United States each year.

The Zapatista Rebellion

The people of Chiapas are among the poorest in all of Mexico. Most belong to indigenous groups and feel little connection with Mexico as a whole. Chiapas has few schools or hospitals. About 90 percent of its indigenous people do not have electricity or running water. On January 1, 1994, a guerrilla army launched an armed rebellion in Chiapas. The group called itself the Zapatista National Liberation Army, taking the name of the revolutionary hero Emiliano Zapata. Fighting for the rights of the impoverished, the Zapatistas won international sympathy. As a result of the rebellion, the Mexican government allowed the people of Chiapas greater political freedom. Local leaders were given funds to provide more services to the people.

Texas and the southwestern United States. The warfare over narcotics is largely confined to Mexico's northern states, but it hurts tourism throughout the country. Many potential tourists read newspaper headlines concerning drug violence and assume that all of Mexico is dangerous.

The year 2010 was special to Mexicans. It marked the hundredth anniversary of the beginning of the Mexican Revolution and the two hundredth birthday of the independence movement. Mexicans threw a vast party, or fiesta, for themselves. Fiestas are a grand tradition in Mexico. The Mexican writer and philosopher Octavio Paz once observed, "If we hide ourselves in our daily lives, we discharge ourselves in the whirlwind of the fiesta." The nationwide party began on the night of September 15, just before Independence Day. In cities and towns rockets flared, bands played, and people shouted into the night, "*¡Viva México! ¡Viva México!*" Long live Mexico!

A fireworks display lights the sky above Mexico City during the nation's bicentennial celebration.

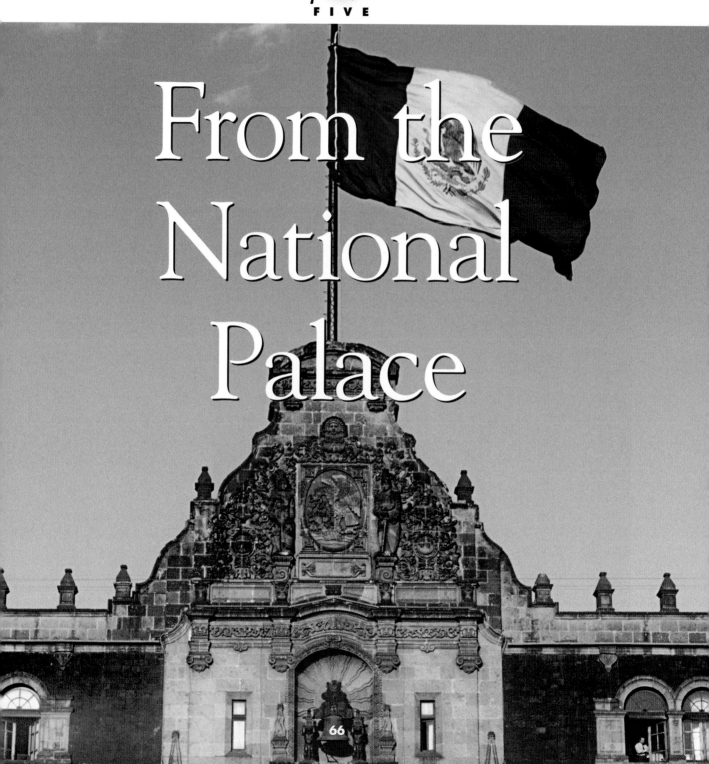

From the National Palace

M EXICO IS GOVERNED BY THE CONSTITUTION OF 1917. At the time it was written, Mexico was in the throes of the revolution of 1910. Despite the warfare, a congress met in the city of Querétaro to write a new constitution. The congress hoped to create a document that would guide the nation by rule of law and end its long history of military revolts and civil wars. In many respects the writers of the constitution achieved their goal. Since the end of the revolution in 1920, Mexico has never again had a violent change of government.

Opposite: **The president's offices are in the National Palace, a grand building in the center of Mexico City.**

The Workings of Government

The constitution of 1917 made Mexico a democracy and a federal republic. Mexico has a federal government, thirty-one state governments, and one federal district. Each of these government bodies is headed by a group of elected officials. All Mexican citizens age eighteen and older are entitled to vote. The constitution guarantees land, labor, education, and health rights for citizens and greatly restricts the activities of the Roman Catholic Church in the nation.

Meet the President

Felipe Calderón was born in 1962 in the state of Michoacán. His father was an important political leader. In 2006, Calderón ran for president. He won by less than 1 percent of the votes cast. This was the narrowest margin of victory for any president in Mexican history. Calderón's opponent, Andrés Manuel López Obrador, insisted that he, Obrador, had won the election. For several tense weeks, both men claimed the presidency. In the past, this situation could have triggered a civil war. But Mexicans have acquired political maturity. Felipe Calderón peacefully took the oath of office on December 1, 2006. Early in his term he announced a crackdown on the drug trade in northern Mexico. In effect, the president declared war on the drug gangs. The conflict has been brutal. On January 25, 2011, Mexico City's English-language newspaper,

the *News*, reported, "More than 34,600 people have died in drug-related killings in Mexico in the four years since Calderón launched his drug offensive."

Mexico's congress, or lawmaking body, is divided into two houses, the Senate and the Chamber of Deputies. The Senate has 128 members and the Chamber of Deputies has 500 members. Senators are elected to six-year terms, and deputies serve three-year terms.

Mexico's president holds the most important and powerful office in the nation. The president serves one six-year term and cannot be reelected. New laws are often introduced by the president and are later put into effect by the congress. This process is the reverse of the way bills become law in the United States. In the United States, Congress introduces and passes bills, which are then signed into law by the president.

The Mexican president names his or her own cabinet. Each cabinet minister heads a department within the government. Cabinet ministers are sometimes very powerful. For example, the secretary of the interior acts as the nation's leading police officer and has wide latitude to enforce the law.

Under special circumstances, the president has

NATIONAL GOVERNMENT OF MEXICO

Executive Branch

PRESIDENT

CABINET

Legislative Branch

SENATE
(128 MEMBERS)

CHAMBER OF DEPUTIES
(500 MEMBERS)

Judicial Branch

SUPREME COURT OF JUSTICE

Senators serve six-year terms and are not allowed to serve two terms in a row.

A group of schoolchildren tour the National Palace, where the president works. The building was constructed on the site of Montezuma's palace.

the power to remove and replace a state governor. The writers of the constitution deliberately gave the president greater authority than the heads of the states. They hoped that rule by one person would promote national stability. According to the constitution of 1917, the president has "broad power of appointment and removal, fiscal powers, the power to veto legislation, and control of the military."

The Flag of Mexico

In the center of the flag of Mexico is a picture of an eagle perched on a cactus while eating a snake. This image is a tribute to the Aztec legend about the founding of Tenochtitlán, today's Mexico City. The flag also has three stripes. The green stripe represents independence, the white stripe stands for the purity of the Roman Catholic faith, and the red stripe represents the blood shed by the nation's heroes.

The National Anthem

The lyrics of Mexico's national anthem, or "El Himno Nacional," were written in 1853 by a poet named Francisco González Bocanegra. The following year, Jaime Nunó set the lyrics to music. The song was officially adopted as the national anthem in 1943. Here is an English translation:

Chorus:
Mexicans, at the cry of war,
Make ready the steel and the bridle,
And the earth trembles at its centers
At the resounding roar of the cannon
And the earth trembles at its centers
At the resounding roar of the cannon.

First Verse:
Let gird, o fatherland, your brow with olive
By the divine archangel of peace
For in heaven your eternal destiny
Was written by the finger of God.
But if some enemy outlander should dare
To profane your ground with his step,
Think, o beloved fatherland, that heaven
Has given you a soldier in every son.

The highest court in Mexico is the Supreme Court of Justice. This court has eleven justices and one chief justice, all of whom are nominated by the president and must be approved by the Senate. Each state has its own court system headed by its own state supreme court.

Courts in Mexico have limited power. The court system almost always supports the actions of the president.

The Rights of the People

Under the constitution of 1917, the federal government has a responsibility to promote the well-being of the people. The constitution contains language granting the Mexican people social, economic, and cultural rights. It was the first constitution of any nation to guarantee certain privileges to individuals. The right to education is guaranteed by the

Union members hold a protest demanding that a mining company fix its safety violations. Mexico's constitution gives people the right to form labor unions.

constitution. Freedom of religion was made a rule of law, ending the Catholic Church's grip on Mexico. One article in the constitution grants people the right to form labor unions and another prohibits child labor. Unfortunately, some of the lofty goals of the constitution have not been put into practice. Child labor, for example, is still a sad reality in Mexico.

President Felipe Calderón is a member of the National Action Party (Partido de Acción Nacional, or PAN). His party membership alone represents a positive change in Mexican political life. For generations Mexico was a one-party nation. The only party with political power was the Institutional Revolutionary Party (Partido Revolucionario Institucional, or PRI). The

A woman casts her vote. Mexicans must be at least eighteen years old to vote.

Groundbreaking Governor

Historically, Mexican women have had little involvement in government and politics. Women did not gain the right to vote in Mexico until 1953. In most other nations, women won this right early in the twentieth century. In 1979, Griselda Álvarez became Mexico's first female governor. She was elected to the office in the state of Colima. Álvarez was also a teacher, a writer, and a noted poet. As governor she emphasized education and launched a program called Educar Para Progresar (Educate for Progress).

PRI originated in 1929, and for the next seventy-one years all presidents were party members. Most state governors were also PRI loyalists.

Great change came to Mexico in the year 2000, when Vicente Fox was elected president. Fox was a member of PAN. At last the hold of the PRI over Mexico had been broken.

To many observers the change from one-party rule was astonishing. The PRI had become an arm of the government. Critics said that the party was the government itself. Any young person interested in becoming a political leader had to win the approval of party regulars. Many of these party regulars were corrupt and hungry for power. The opening of the political process was hailed as one of the most constructive developments in the history of modern Mexico.

Today, Mexico is a multiparty democracy. The PRI remains the major party, with most of the seats in the national congress. PAN is the second most popular political party. Other important parties include a green party, which emphasizes environmental issues, and a labor party, which reaches out to working men and women.

The Bustling Capital

Aztec stories say that the city of Tenochtitlán was founded in 1325. The nation's capital, called Mexico City, was built on this same spot. Sitting in the Mexican Plateau at an elevation of 7,349 feet (2,240 m) above sea level, Mexico City is the highest big city in North America. In 2009, Mexico City had a population of 12,294,193. But that does not tell the whole story. With some 22 million people packed into its sprawling metropolitan area, Mexico City is one of the largest cities on earth. About 270,000 people move to Mexico City each year, so the city continues to grow. Mexico City struggles with traffic congestion and air pollution.

The people of Mexico City often escape the crowded streets by heading to one of the city's many parks. Sometimes one million people visit Chapultepec Park on Sunday. Some also visit the National Museum of Anthropology and History located in the park, where they can learn more about Mexico's ancient cultures.

At the center of the city is a large plaza called the Zócalo. Some of the nation's most important buildings flank the Zócalo, including the National Cathedral (below) and the National Palace, the president's office. In many ways, the Zócalo is the center of the nation. When Mexicans want to make their frustrations heard, they hold demonstrations in the Zócalo.

Beautiful tree-lined streets cut through historic neighborhoods in the city center, such as Coyoacán and San Ángel. In these neighborhoods, well-off Mexicans live in modern apartment buildings or old houses, rich in architectural detail.

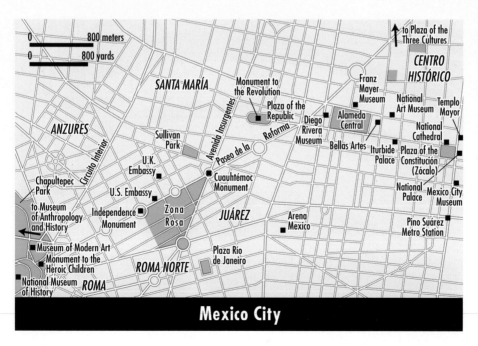

Mexico City

Selling and Buying

I N 2010, WORKERS IN THE MEXICO CITY SUBURB OF Nezahualcóyotl set up a large tent. Inside were rows of tables with folding chairs. The occasion was a job fair sponsored by the local government. On the opening day, thousands of eager young job seekers poured into the tent. Carefully they studied lists of job openings—security guard, delivery-truck driver, cashier at a new Walmart store. The best-paying offers promised a salary of about five thousand pesos a month (roughly four hundred U.S. dollars). This isn't much, because the prices for staple items such as soap and toothpaste are almost as high in Mexico as they are in the United States and Canada. Despite the meager pay, the men and women inquired eagerly about each position. In Mexico a job—any kind of job—is golden.

Modern Mexico suffers from a dire problem. It has far more workers than it has jobs. Mexico is a young country. The average age for a Mexican man or woman is 27.1 years. A huge percentage of the population is under the age of 15. Every year more than a million young people leave school and enter the job market. There simply are not enough jobs for so many young workers.

Opposite: **Cowboy hats are among the many goods sold in the Artisans' Market in San Miguel de Allende.**

Women set up fruit and vegetables at an outdoor market in Chiapas, in southern Mexico.

The Agricultural Economy

Throughout most of Mexico's history, its economy was based on farming. Farmers raised corn, beans, chili peppers, and other vegetables. They usually kept a few pigs and chickens as well. Farmers sold their produce at local markets.

Life under the old system was unfair, because a few wealthy landowners held the most productive farmland. The average farmer, or *campesino*, raised food for himself and his family and earned very little. Still, the small farmers felt strong, lasting ties with the land. During the government of Porfirio Díaz (1876–1911), wealthy Mexicans and foreigners seized lands and forced the people to work for them. The revolution was an effort to change this practice. The land reform program returned it to the people, who worked it in communal properties called the *ejido*.

After World War II, thousands of factories opened in the cities. People left the farms to take jobs making shoes, clothing, or fertilizers. These people left the countryside because there was not enough good farmland for the growing population. The farming tradition, which was as old as Mexico itself, changed radically.

In 2010 the Mexican government claimed the country had an unemployment rate of 5.6 percent. This is less than the U.S. jobless rate, but the figure does not give a true picture. The government considers a person who shines shoes at a public park to be employed, though earnings from a shoe

Neza

Nezahualcóyotl is named for a poet from Texcoco from the time of the Aztecs. The city illustrates Mexico's changing economy and the people's rush to the cities. In 1950, Nezahualcóyotl, which lies near Mexico City's main airport, was a patch of barren ground with a few scattered houses. The expansion of factory jobs brought millions of people into Mexico City from the countryside. In less than two decades, Nezahualcóyotl had more than one million people and had become the tenth-largest urban area in all of Mexico. At first the town was a desperate slum without schools, housing, or adequate sanitation. Gradually, however, the residents planted gardens and built better homes. Many now give their town the affectionate name "Neza."

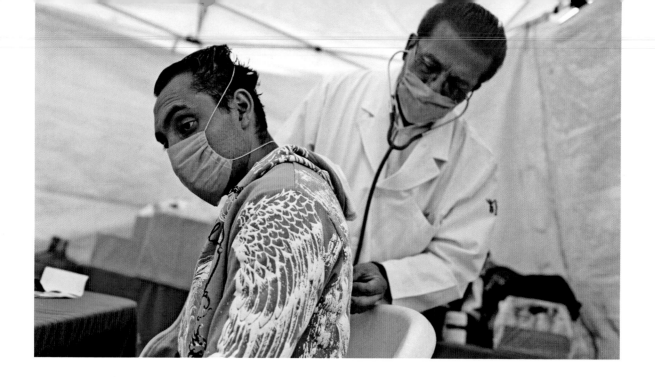

A doctor checks a patient for flu symptoms. More than 60 percent of Mexicans have jobs in service industries such as medicine.

shine stand amount to very little. A truer measure of workers' lives is the poverty rate. This figure compares earnings to everyday expenses such as food. The U.S. government says that 47 percent of Mexicans live below the poverty line, meaning that almost half of the Mexican people struggle to meet basic needs. They have almost no money to spare for things that are not necessities.

Carlos Slim Helú

While masses of Mexicans live in poverty, the nation supports a large upper class. Among its members is Carlos Slim Helú, the son of Lebanese immigrants who came to Mexico in the early 1900s. Investing mainly in Mexican telephone companies, Slim amassed a staggering fortune worth more than fifty billion U.S. dollars. In 2010, the U.S. publication *Forbes* named Slim the richest person on earth.

Money Facts

Mexico's currency is the peso, which literally means "weight." The term stems from the weight of silver or gold coins. In 2011, 11.7 pesos equaled one U.S. dollar.

The most widely used bill in Mexico is the twenty-peso note, known simply as *el veinte*, the twenty. It bears a picture of President Benito Juárez on one side. U.S. tourists generally think of the twenty-peso note as worth two dollars, though it is actually valued somewhat less than that. The highest bill in use in Mexico is worth one thousand pesos. The coin most widely used is worth ten pesos, or about one dollar in the United States.

Where the Jobs Are

The Mexican workforce numbers forty-seven million men and women. Mexico has the thirteenth-largest labor force in the world. Jobs are divided into three broad categories: services (which employ 62.9 percent of Mexico's workers), industry (23.4 percent), and agriculture (13.7 percent).

Service Jobs

The majority of the Mexican people are employed in service jobs. A service worker performs a job that involves doing things for others rather than making products. A teacher is a service worker. So are a doctor, a taxi driver, and a bank teller. Most service jobs in Mexico pay low wages. For instance, private house cleaners may earn as little as fifty pesos a day. In Mexico City, fifty pesos is enough to buy a Big Mac and fries

A man works on an assembly line building Volkswagen Beetles. Mexico is the tenth-largest producer of cars in the world.

at a neighborhood McDonald's. A house cleaner could work all day and spend the entire day's pay on one lunch.

Manufacturing

People who work in factories generally earn more than service employees do. Major Mexican industries produce processed foods and beverages, chemical products, iron and steel, and automobiles and trucks. The output of Mexican factories rises and falls with the worldwide economy. The global recession that struck in 2008 cut the worldwide demand for goods and slowed Mexico's industrial economy.

Maquiladoras

About 1.3 million Mexicans hold jobs in factories on the Mexican side of the U.S.-Mexican border. Mexican factory workers earn considerably less than their U.S. counterparts. Overall, the Mexican pay scale is about one-third that of the United States. Eager to take advantage of the lower wages, investors built factories, called *maquiladoras*, along the border. Because they provided jobs, the maquiladoras met with approval from the Mexican government. The maquiladoras churned out mass-produced items such as radios, televisions, and washing machines. After the year 2000 they began to face steep competition. Factories in Indonesia and China produced goods even more cheaply than those in Mexico. Indonesian and Chinese workers earned still less than Mexican workers.

To most Mexicans, factory work is desirable employment. It is steady and it pays relatively well. But factory jobs are difficult to obtain. The city of Monterrey in the north is an industrial center with some five hundred factories. Yet many people in Monterrey sell newspapers or peddle candy bars because they cannot find work in an industrial plant.

Agriculture

Farming, once the economic backbone of Mexico, is now the weakest section of the economy. Only 12 percent of Mexico's total land area is devoted to farming. Corn is the food product

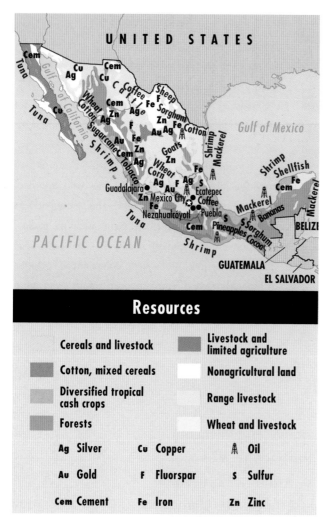

Resources

Cereals and livestock

Livestock and limited agriculture

Cotton, mixed cereals

Nonagricultural land

Diversified tropical cash crops

Range livestock

Forests

Wheat and livestock

Ag Silver Cu Copper Oil

Au Gold F Fluorspar S Sulfur

Cem Cement Fe Iron Zn Zinc

in greatest demand among the people. Early in the 1970s Mexico began importing corn to meet the demand. The government has long favored policies that spur the growth of industry, while allowing the agricultural economy to sag.

Mexican farmers raise corn, wheat, rice, beans, cotton, coffee, and fruit. They also raise livestock, including poultry and beef cattle. Hired farmhands are among the most poorly paid members of the workforce.

The Economic Picture

One measure of a nation's economy is the gross domestic product (GDP). The GDP combines the value of all of the goods made by the nation in a given year. In 2010 the U.S. government measured Mexico's GDP at 1.56 trillion U.S. dollars. This figure ranked Mexico as the twelfth-largest economy in the world.

For years, tourism remained the brightest spot on Mexico's economic horizon. Tourism created more jobs than any other industry in the nation. Tourist hotels and restaurants tended to employ low-wage service workers. Jobs in tourism depend on the number of foreign visitors. In 2009 and 2010, the

Men harvest tangerines in eastern Mexico, where most of the nation's citrus fruit is grown.

What Mexico Grows, Makes, and Mines

Agriculture (2008)

Sugarcane	51 million metric tons
Corn	24 million metric tons
Milk	11 million metric tons

Manufacturing (2007, value in Mexican pesos)

Foods and beverages	994,797,000,000
Transportation equipment	146,839,000,000
Chemicals	125,629,000,000

Mining

Oil	3.7 million barrels per day
Zinc	410,000 metric tons
Silver	3,085 metric tons

A train crosses a high bridge in central Mexico.

tourist industry slowed in several regions of Mexico. Foreigners feared that the drug wars, which generally took place in the north, made the whole country unsafe.

Mining and natural resources are also important to the economy in Mexico. Oil wells pump three million barrels of crude oil a day, making Mexico the seventh-largest oil producer in the world. Mexico ranks fifteenth worldwide in the production of natural gas. It is one of the largest silver producers in the world. Silver from Mexico is minted into coins and also has industrial uses.

Mexico has well-developed transportation and communication systems. The country has 10,877 miles (17,505 km) of railroad tracks, ranking it sixteenth in the world in rail transport. About 19,000 miles (30,000 km) of highways serve the nation. Almost twenty million telephones are in regular use, and some thirty-one million Mexicans use the Internet. In many of Mexico's rural areas, telephone landlines are not yet available. People who lack phone access visit Internet cafés, where they can go online for a few pesos and communicate with their far-flung friends and family.

Education

Mexico's economic prospects are closely linked to education. The Mexican government has made a major effort to educate the nation's young people. Today, 98 percent of all Mexicans between the ages of fifteen and twenty-four can read and write. This figure shows a dramatic change from earlier years, when children in rural areas had very limited opportunities to attend school. Mexico's push toward education helps ensure that Mexicans will be prepared to compete in the world market of the future.

Students in Mexico are required to go to school through at least age fifteen.

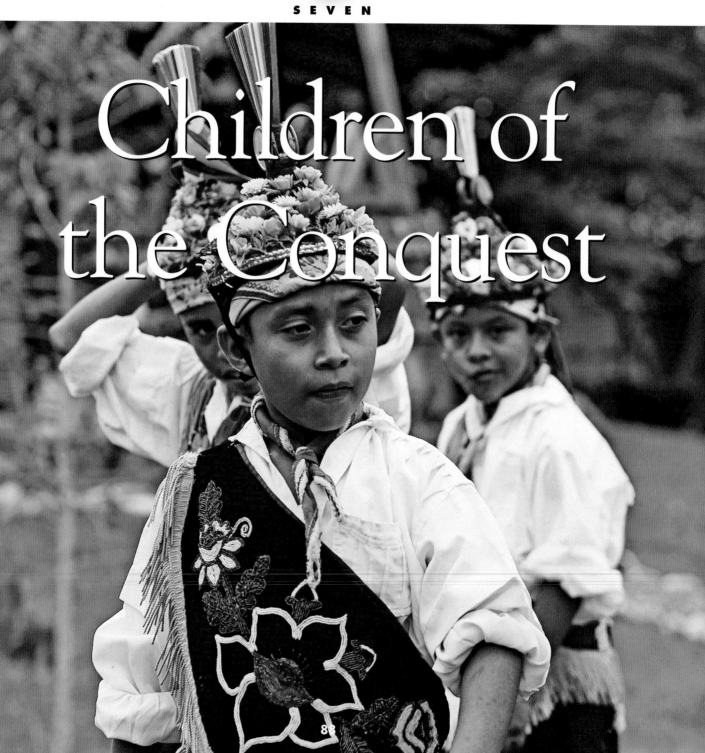

Children of the Conquest

SOON AFTER HERNÁN CORTÉS ARRIVED IN MEXICO, HE met a young Mayan woman called Malinalli. Malinalli had a gift for languages, and she soon became Cortés's interpreter. She was at his side when he met with the Aztec emperor, Montezuma. Eventually Cortés and Malinalli had a son, one of the first children born in Mexico of Spanish and indigenous parents.

Today Mexicans sometimes refer to Malinalli, or La Malinche, as a traitor to her people. She acted against the Aztecs and helped Cortés carry out his conquest. At the same time, she is seen as the mother of Mexico's mixed race people, the mestizos.

Opposite: **Mexican boys perform a ritual dance.**

Spanish Names

Spanish names can be confusing to foreigners. In Mexico and other Spanish-speaking countries, it is common for a person to use two last names. The father's last name comes first, followed by the mother's last name. If a girl is named Julia López Rodríguez, her father's last name is López and her mother's last name is Rodríguez. If Julia marries Antonio González Sánchez, she will add de González to her name and become Julia López Rodríguez de González. Her children's names will end with González López.

Teenagers in the state of Sinaloa, on the Pacific coast.

Spanish Pronunciation

Here are the sounds of the vowels in Spanish:

a	ah
e	eh
i	ee
o	oh
u	oo

Black Mexicans

During the three centuries of colonial rule, between 1521 and 1821, about two hundred thousand Africans were brought to Mexico to serve as slaves. Mexico abolished slavery when it won its independence from Spain. Today people of African heritage live chiefly along Mexico's Gulf Coast and in Acapulco on the Pacific.

Spanish Phrases

Here are a few phrases that may come in handy if you visit Mexico or are speaking to a Mexican visitor in the United States.

¿Cómo te llamas?	(¿CO-mo teh YAH-mahs?)	What is your name?
Me llamo Pablo.	(Meh YAH-mo PAB-loh.)	My name is Pablo.
¿Cuántos años tiene usted?	(¿QUAHN-tos AHN-yos ti-EH-ne oos-TED?)	How old are you? (Literally, this question asks, how many years do you have?)
Yo tengo doce años.	(Yo TEN-go DO-ceh AHN-yos.)	I am twelve years old. (Literally, the answer is, I have twelve years.)

Ethnic Groups and Languages

Mestizos comprise about 60 percent of Mexico's population today. About 30 percent of Mexico's people are indigenous, and approximately 9 percent are of European ancestry. The remaining 1 percent of people are listed as "other," which includes Asians and people of African descent.

A legacy of the conquest, Spanish is the official language of Mexico. Mexico is the largest Spanish-speaking nation in the world. In English, each vowel (*a*, *e*, *i*, *o*, and *u*) has several distinct pronunciations. Spanish is much simpler in this regard. Each of its vowels has only one sound. An accent sign

Ethnic Mexico

Mestizos	60%
Indigenous people	30%
Caucasians	9%
Other	1%

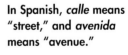

In Spanish, *calle* means "street," and *avenida* means "avenue."

Largest Indigenous Language Groups in Mexico

- Nahua (Aztec)
- Maya
- Zapotec
- Mixtec
- Totonac
- Purépecha

Speakers of Indigenous Languages

Nahua (Aztec)	1.7 million
Maya	1 million
Zapotec	500,000
Mixtec	500,000
Totonac	260,000
Purépecha	130,000

over a vowel indicates the strongest syllable in a word. A mark, called a tilde, placed over the letter *n* gives it the sound "ny," as in the word *piñata*. The double *ll* in Spanish is pronounced much like the English letter *y*. Thus the word *llama* is pronounced "yama." The Spanish letter *j* has a sound not used in English. It is something like a raspy letter *h*. And here's one more thing to remember—the *h* in Spanish is always silent.

Many different indigenous languages are spoken in Mexico. More than three million Mexicans speak an indigenous language. Most of these indigenous speakers also speak some Spanish.

The Mexican government recognizes fifty-six indigenous groups living within the country. Most indigenous communities survive in rural areas with few roads, schools, or other connections to the outside world. As roads and electricity begin to link these communities to towns and cities, indigenous people start to move toward the mainstream culture. Young people watch television, visit Web sites, and study Spanish in school. As a result, many of Mexico's native languages are disappearing.

A Swelling Population

In 2010 Mexico had a population of approximately 113.7 million and growing. Some demographers, or population experts, predict that Mexico's population will double by 2060. The main reason for Mexico's population growth is that people are living longer than ever before, while the country's birthrate has remained the same. Improved nutrition, better medical care, and better sanitation have all helped people live longer, healthier lives. Widespread immunization against killer diseases such as smallpox, measles, and diphtheria have also cut Mexico's death rate in the past fifty years.

Until the 1960s, Mexico was an agricultural society. The majority of the people lived on farms or in small villages. But as Mexico's population has grown, the country has experienced a vast internal movement of people, or migration. Each year hundreds of thousands of people leave rural areas to look for jobs in the cities. By 2010, about 77 percent of all Mexicans lived in urban areas. This migration out of rural areas is expected to continue, so Mexico's cities will continue to expand.

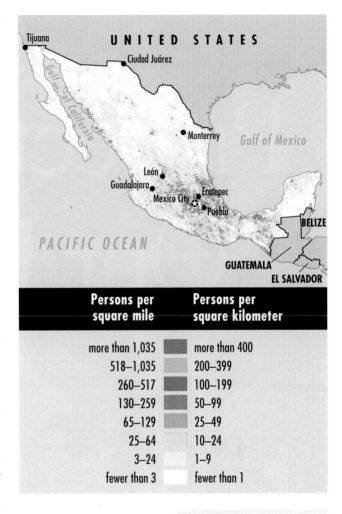

Persons per square mile	Persons per square kilometer
more than 1,035	more than 400
518–1,035	200–399
260–517	100–199
130–259	50–99
65–129	25–49
25–64	10–24
3–24	1–9
fewer than 3	fewer than 1

Population of Major Cities (2009)

Mexico City	12,294,193
Ecatepec	1,806,226
Guadalajara	1,640,589
Puebla	1,590,256
Ciudad Juárez	1,512,354

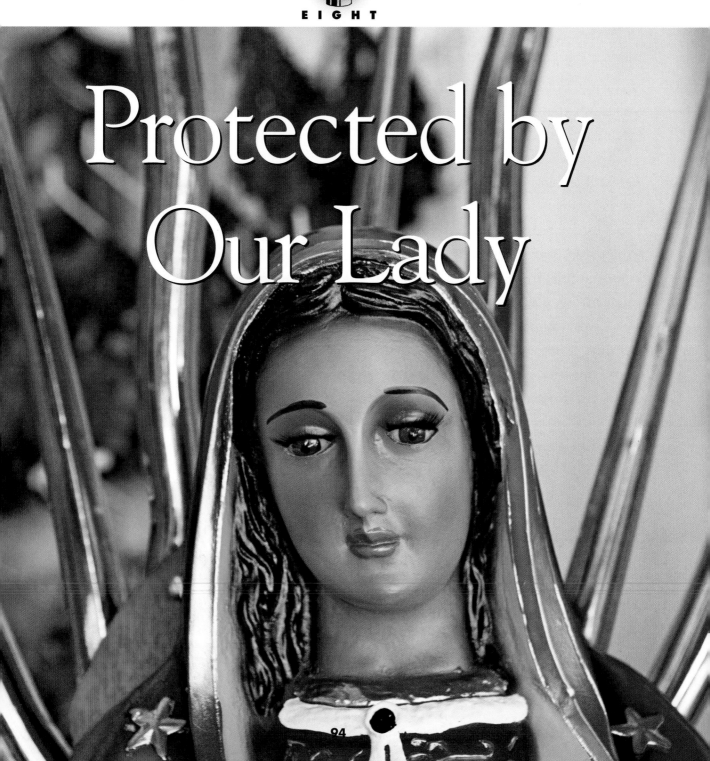

Protected by Our Lady

94

ON DECEMBER 9, 1531, TEN YEARS AFTER THE SPANISH conquest of Mexico, an Indian named Juan Diego climbed Tepeyac Hill near Mexico City. Suddenly he saw a beautiful lady. She told him to tell the Roman Catholic bishop to build a church on the spot where she stood. Juan Diego begged her to send someone else. He was convinced that the bishop would not listen to him. But the lady insisted that he must be her messenger. "I am the Mother of all of you who dwell in this land," she explained.

Juan Diego carried the lady's message to the bishop. Just as he feared, the bishop did not take him seriously. Two more times, the lady appeared and sent Juan Diego to the bishop. Finally, the bishop told Juan Diego to bring him proof of what he had seen.

Juan Diego returned to Tepeyac Hill and once again met the lovely lady. This time she told him to pick some roses and wrap them in his *tilma*, or woven cape. The bishop was astonished to see the roses, which did not usually grow in that region. He was even more amazed when he discovered, painted on Juan Diego's tilma, the portrait of a beautiful dark-

Opposite: **Images of Our Lady of Guadalupe are seen everywhere in Mexico.**

Protected by Our Lady **95**

A Mexican Saint

For centuries scholars and religious leaders have wondered about Juan Diego and the mysterious painting. Some claim that the painting was really the work of an Aztec artist called Marcus. Others point out that in five hundred years the fabric on which the portrait is painted has never crumbled. Surely, they say, this proves that Juan Diego witnessed a miracle. In 2002, the Roman Catholic Church declared Juan Diego to be a saint. He is called St. Juan Diego Cuauhtlatoatzín.

skinned lady. Convinced that a miracle had taken place, he ordered the church to be built.

The lady said to have come to Juan Diego is known throughout Mexico and the world as Our Lady of Guadalupe. Today she is considered the patron saint of Mexico and the Americas. In Mexico her presence seems to be everywhere, and four, the number of her appearances to Juan Diego, is a lucky number. Her image hangs in fancy shops and humble homes. It can be seen on buses, in factories, and in doctors' offices. She is the protector of all Mexico. The nation's mestizos and indigenous people especially revere her.

A Catholic Nation

Religions in Mexico	
Roman Catholic	89%
Protestant	6%
Other	5%

In every Mexican village and town, the pealing of church bells is woven into everyday life. At six o'clock in the morning the bells call the faithful to mass. They ring again at noon, and again at sundown. Church bells clamor with joy at weddings and christenings, and toll for the dead when a funeral occurs.

About 89 percent of all Mexicans are Roman Catholic. Catholic beliefs and customs are part of everyday life throughout the country. A bus driver makes the sign of the cross as he sets off down the highway. The statues of saints stand in gardens and patios. When people make plans together, they might say, "I'll see you Friday, *si dios quiere*," (if God wills).

Many pilgrims who visit the Basilica of Guadalupe carry images of Our Lady of Guadalupe with them.

Protestants make up about 6 percent of Mexico's population. Several Protestant groups, including Seventh-Day Adventists, Pentecostals, and Mormons, work actively to win Mexican converts. Mexico also has small Jewish and Muslim communities, mostly in the major cities.

The Basilica of Guadalupe

Each year millions of visitors flock to the Basilica of Guadalupe in Mexico City to see the famous painting of Our Lady of Guadalupe, Mexico's patron saint. The basilica receives more visitors than any other Roman Catholic shrine in the world.

Built near the site of a sixteenth-century church, the new basilica was completed in 1976. On the grounds stands the original chapel that was built in the 1500s after Our Lady of Guadalupe was said to have appeared to Juan Diego.

Gods and Goddesses

Here are some of the gods and goddesses worshipped by indigenous peoples before the Spaniards arrived:

Centeotl—god of corn

Ehecatl—god of wind

Tlaloc—god of rain (right)

Tonantzín—goddess of the earth

Tonatiuh—god of the sun

Xochiquetzal—goddess of flowers

Gods and Saints

Although Mexico is a heavily Catholic country, Mexican Catholicism is laced with elements from older traditions. The Aztecs and other native peoples worshipped hundreds of gods and goddesses. They represented plants, animals, and other aspects of the natural world. After the Spanish conquest, the saints of the Roman Catholic Church replaced the gods that

Ehecatl, the Aztec god of wind, is shown with a bird beak.

the native people had worshipped. Often the indigenous people gave traits of their old gods to the new Catholic saints. In many ways Our Lady of Guadalupe resembles Tonantzín, the Aztec goddess of the earth. In fact, the first church to Our Lady of Guadalupe was built where Tonantzín's temple once stood.

Celebrating the Saints

Throughout the year, Mexico's calendar is dotted with saints' days and other religious holidays. Christmas, Easter, and Corpus Christi are the major holidays. Candelaria, February 2, marks the beginning of spring planting. In many towns vendors set up stalls selling a dazzling variety of plants and flowers. The feast day of St. John, or San Juan, is celebrated on June 24, and St. Michael, or San Miguel, is honored on September 29. Our Lady of Guadalupe has her special celebration on December 12. The feast days of dozens of other saints are also treated as special occasions. Saints' days are celebrated with processions, music, fireworks, and the ringing of church bells.

San Juan de los Lagos

Every year in late January more than a million people from all over Mexico visit the town of San Juan de los Lagos in the state of Jalisco. A church in San Juan houses a small statue of the Virgin Mary that is believed to perform miraculous cures. Thousands of pilgrims make the journey to San Juan on foot, walking for ten days or more to worship at the shrine.

From Hands, Hearts, and Minds

E ACH YEAR SOME TWO MILLION VISITORS PASS THROUGH the halls of Mexico's National Museum of Anthropology and History. Founded in 1964, the museum houses a stunning collection of carvings, jewelry, and architectural models that represent the work of Mexico's pre-Columbian peoples. The museum's vast exhibits show that artistic expression has been part of Mexican life for more than a thousand years.

Opposite: **This Mayan head was found in a burial chamber at Palenque, in southern Mexico.**

Written in Stone

The ancient Maya of Yucatán created monumental stone sculptures known as stelae. Some stelae weigh as much as 60 tons (54 metric tons). The stelae were covered with carvings of rulers and gods. Many include inscriptions in the written language of the Maya. These inscriptions have helped scientists learn a great deal about Maya life and beliefs.

The Maya also carved small stone figures and made beautiful jade and silver jewelry. They made lovely ceramic bowls and vases, which were decorated with detailed paintings of people and animals. The Maya made dyes from plant leaves

How Did They Do It?

To this day, no one knows how the Maya transported massive stones from faraway quarries to their cities in the rain forest. The Maya had no horses, oxen, or other beasts of burden. They did not have wheeled carts or wagons. How they moved such huge stones is yet another mystery.

and powdered clay. A pigment called Maya blue came from the leaves of the indigo plant.

Like the Maya, the Aztecs used art to celebrate their gods and rulers. They decorated their temples with stone statues of the gods and goddesses. They also carved small figures of animals and humans from jade and quartz. Obsidian, or volcanic glass, occurs in several colors, especially black, and the Aztecs used it for jewelry, mirrors, and even surgical knives.

The Calendar Stone

The Aztec Calendar Stone is one of the most remarkable examples of pre-Columbian art in Mexico. It weighs 24 tons (22 metric tons) and measures 12 feet (3.7 m) across. At the center is the carved face of Tonatiuh, the Aztec sun god. Surrounding the god's face are circles marked to show the days of the year. The Calendar Stone is one of the most prized exhibits at the National Museum of Anthropology and History.

Many Mexican pots are large and colorful.

Useful and Beautiful

Many Mexican objects are both useful and beautiful. Belts, bags, bowls, and baskets are made by highly skilled men and women trained in traditional crafts. People all over the world treasure Mexican crafts.

Many Mexican artisans make ceramic pottery. There is tremendous variety in the pottery, with each region producing its own patterns. Potters make cups, dishes, pitchers, and giant planters.

The streets of Dolores Hidalgo are lined with workshops where ceramic tiles are made and painted. Before the clay tiles are fired in a kiln to make them hard, they are spread out in the sun to dry. Sometimes a wandering dog leaves its footprints on the tile, and the tracks are preserved when the tile goes into the kiln. If you look carefully, you may see dog prints scattered across the walls and ceiling of a Mexican house.

Some towns and regions are noted for particular crafts. Tlaquepaque, outside Guadalajara, is known for its glassware, Pátzcuaro is famous for lacquered wooden boxes, and Saltillo has a reputation for its serapes, blanketlike shawls. The state of Michoacán is renowned for its fine guitars and other musical instruments. The Seri Indian women of Sonora make tightly woven baskets from the fibers of a shrub called the limberbush. The Seris also carve masks and animal figures from a dense, hard wood called ironwood.

The Fine Arts

Mexicans excel in every branch of the arts, from painting and sculpture to photography and filmmaking. Their most outstanding contribution has been in the realm of the mural,

Pictures in Yarn

The Huichol Indians of Jalisco and Nayarit create pictures by pressing colored yarn into beeswax on a square or oblong board. During the 1960s, a Huichol named Ramón Medina Silva developed this art form, which became a source of income for his people. The yarn paintings depict traditional Huichol religious symbols and images of the gods.

or large wall painting. During the twentieth century Mexico produced three muralists known as world masters. The Big Three, as they are often called, are David Alfaro Siqueiros, José Clemente Orozco, and Diego Rivera.

The three great muralists emerged in the era after the Mexican Revolution and did most of their murals during the 1920s and 1930s. They used their art as a way to educate the Mexican people and to give them a sense of pride in their

Detail of *Dream of a Sunday Afternoon*, by Diego Rivera. The entire mural is 50 feet (15 m) long.

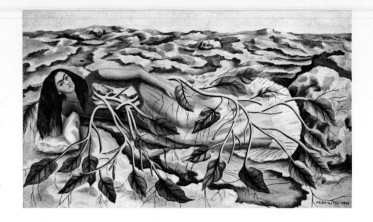

Frida Kahlo

Diego Rivera's wife, Frida Kahlo (1907–1954), is one of Mexico's most beloved artists. She began painting after she was severely injured in a bus accident when she was eighteen. Many of her paintings are self-portraits. They reflect the pain of her injuries as well as her delight in the colors of Mexican dress and scenery.

heritage. Both Rivera and Siqueiros tended to glorify the revolution. They showed the Mexican people as noble and heroic. Orozco painted the horrors of war and the threat of dependence on technology.

Music

Many Mexicans celebrate their saint's day rather than their birthday. A saint's day is the feast day of the saint after which the person is named. Whichever day is celebrated, it often begins with a charming tradition. At dawn a band of musicians called mariachis gathers beneath the window of the person to be honored. At a signal, the mariachis begin singing Mexico's traditional birthday song, "Las Mañanitas" ("The Little Mornings"). The song is laced with lyrics about flowers and nightingales. By the time the song is over, the person with the birthday is up and ready to begin the special day.

Mariachi music evolved in western Mexico, especially Jalisco, in the late 1800s. On weekend evenings bands perform on plazas of most towns and cities. At first the musicians used only stringed instruments, but today a typical mariachi

The guitarrón is a large, rounded bass guitar.

band consists of two trumpets, six to eight violins, and a standard guitar. Some uniquely Mexican instruments are also used. A rounded guitar called the *vihuela* sets the rhythm. A large, deep-voiced instrument called the *guitarrón* creates the bass line. A small Mexican harp provides melodic flourishes. Most of the members sing in addition to playing instruments.

Master of the Ranchero

José Alfredo Jiménez was a singer and songwriter in the ranchero style. Before he died at age forty-seven, he composed more than one thousand songs. One of his most beloved songs is "Camino de Guanajuato" ("The Road to Guanajuato"). Every year thousands of visitors go to Dolores Hidalgo to pay their respects at his tomb, which is shaped like a giant sombrero.

Ranchero music uses strings, trumpets, and accordions. Ranchero songs generally deal with love and disappointment. The *corrido* is a ranchero-style ballad about heroes and villains.

Classical music also has a strong tradition in Mexico. Mexican composers wrote sacred choral music as early as the sixteenth century. In the twentieth century Mexican composers used indigenous and popular themes in ballets and symphonies. Carlos Chávez and Silvestre Revueltas are among Mexico's best-known composers.

The Orquesta Sinfónica Nacional (National Symphony Orchestra) was founded in Mexico City in 1881. It performs in the Palace of Fine Arts in Mexico City. Many of its members are graduates of Mexico's finest school of music, the National Conservatory. Other important orchestras in Mexico include the Philharmonic Orchestra of Querétaro, the Symphonic Orchestra of the State of Mexico, and the Symphonic Orchestra of Yucatán.

Mexico's Tenor

Plácido Domingo was born in Spain and moved to Mexico with his family when he was a small child. His parents were musicians, and they encouraged his love of singing from an early age. He began his career as a tenor with the Mexico National Opera in 1959 and launched his international career when he sang with the Dallas Civic Opera in 1961. Domingo is one of the world's leading operatic tenors, and he has made more than one hundred recordings.

Dance

The Spaniards brought many European dances to Mexico, and they quickly became popular. Spanish dances included the *sarabanda*, *contradanza*, and *fandango*. Nearly every region and indigenous group in Mexico had its own forms of dance, often used in sacred ceremonies. Roman Catholic missionaries tried to stamp out these dances by adding Christian themes and elements.

Indigenous dances did not die out, but they took on many European influences. At the same time, Spanish dances in Mexico changed under the indigenous influence. A new mestizo dance took root and flourished.

During the War of Independence, Mexican patriots used folkloric dances to instill in people pride for Mexico's heritage. The *jarabe*, a dance from Jalisco, became a symbol of the indepen-

Performing folk dances is one way Mexicans show pride in their country.

dence movement. Folkloric dance grew very popular after the revolution of 1910. During the 1930s classes across Mexico helped keep folkloric dance alive.

In 1952, a dancer named Amelia Hernández founded a dance company called the Baile Folklórico de México. In 1970, this group became Mexico's official dance company.

Writing It Down

Although the Aztecs and Maya had systems for writing, they preserved their stories and poetry through the oral tradition. Priests memorized poems and legends, which they recited at important ceremonies. After the Spanish conquest, indigenous authors began to write in their native languages, using the alphabet they learned from the Spaniards. The *Chilam Balam* is a series of books written in Mayan in the eighteenth century. The texts discuss medicine, history, the calendar, and prophecies.

The Poet Nun

Sor Juana Inés de la Cruz is one of Mexico's best-loved poets. She was born in 1648, at a time when girls were seldom allowed to receive an education. Nevertheless, she studied on her own and mastered Greek, Latin, and Nahuatl. In 1667, she entered a convent, and she spent the rest of her life as a nun. From behind the convent walls she wrote passionate poetry, often defending a woman's right to freedom and respect. Today, her image appears on Mexico's two hundred-peso note.

El Teatro Juárez

Founded in 1903, the Teatro Juárez (Juárez Theater) in Guanajuato is one of the most frequently photographed buildings in Mexico. The outside is richly adorned with columns and wrought iron. Inside, the theater is decorated with wood carvings and stained glass. The theater hosts a busy schedule of plays and musical events.

During the nineteenth century when Mexico was wracked by wars, great writers emerged. José Joaquín Fernández de Lizardi wrote Latin America's first novel, *The Mangy Parrot* (1816), and later in the century, Manuel Payno wrote *The Bandits of Cold River* (1889–1891). Many fine writers emerged during the revolution of 1910. Mariano Azuela captured the struggles of the revolution in his 1916 novel, *The Underdogs*. Octavio Paz describes Mexico's character in his 1945 book, *The Labyrinth of Solitude*. Noted for his essays, novels, and poetry, Paz was awarded the Nobel Prize in Literature in 1990. Another prominent Mexican writer is Carlos Fuentes. His best-known novels include *The Death of Artemio Cruz* (1962) and *The Old Gringo* (1985).

Sports

When the Mexican soccer team plays in the World Cup tournament, the whole nation watches in breathless excitement. In every shop and café customers gaze at TV screens, cheering or groaning at each play. Soccer, or *fútbol*, is Mexico's national

Soccer is one of the most popular sports in Mexico. Everyone is glued to the TV when the national team (in green) competes in the World Cup.

passion. Every four years the World Cup brings together the world's top teams to determine which will be the champion. In 2010, Mexico beat France and reached the second round, only to be defeated by Argentina. Mexico hosted the tournament in 1970 and 1986, but has yet to win the championship.

Baseball is also a popular sport in Mexico. The sport came to Mexico in the late 1800s, probably brought by railroad workers from the United States. The Mexican Professional Baseball League began with six teams in 1925. Today, the Mexican League has sixteen summer teams and eight winter teams.

Mexicans have achieved great success in cycling and race walking, especially in the Olympics. Lorena Ochoa was ranked as the world's number-one golfer by the Women's Professional Golf Association from 2007 to 2010, when she retired.

The Spaniards brought bullfighting to Mexico in 1526,

Ángel Macías, Champion Child

In the summer of 1957, a team from Monterrey, in northeastern Mexico, competed in the Little League World Series. In the stadium in Williamsport, Pennsylvania, twelve-year-old Ángel Macías pitched a perfect game. "In that moment the only thing I remember is that we won the championship," he recalled years later. "I never knew that I was pitching a perfect game. It never crossed my mind." The team's performance sparked new enthusiasm for baseball throughout Mexico and is celebrated to this day.

All the seats are filled at a bullfight at the Plaza de Toros in Mexico City.

and it remains a popular sport. Dressed in a glittering costume, the fighter, or matador, teases the bull with a red cape and attempts to kill it with a single thrust of his sword. Many people are appalled by the cruelty of this sport, but fans claim it is an art form full of grace and courage.

The Plaza de Toros in Mexico City is the largest bullring in the world. It can seat up to sixty thousand people. Altogether Mexico has 220 bullrings in towns and cities across the country.

Another import from Spain is the popular game of jai alai. Jai alai is played in a walled court, or *cancha*. The ball is thrown with a basket on a stick, called a *cesta*. The ball is thrown against the wall or bounced off the floor. Jai alai is played with dizzying speed. To add to the excitement, spectators place bets on the outcome moment to moment. With the shouts of the crowd, the bets flying back and forth, and the lightning-fast action on the court, a jai alai game is a thrilling spectacle.

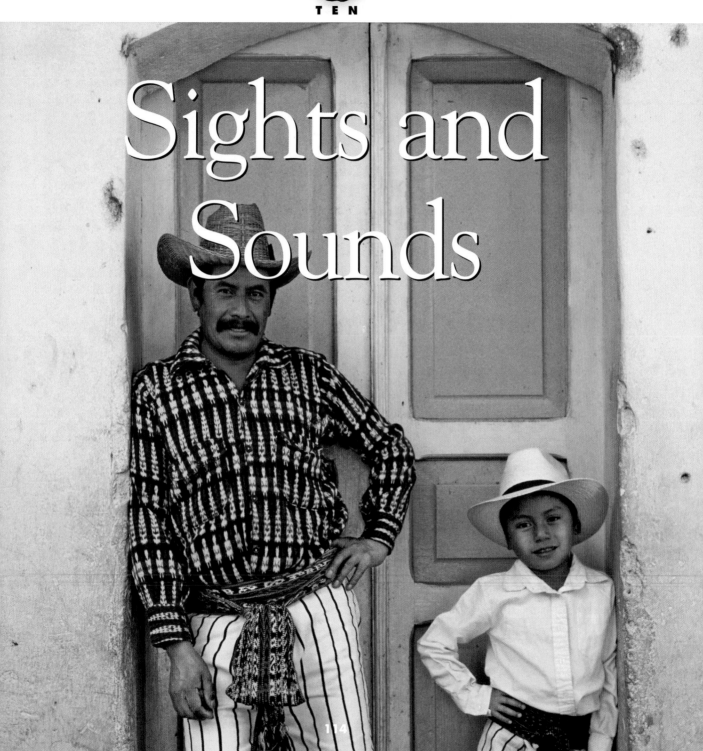

Sights and Sounds

It IS SUNUP IN A TOWN ON THE MEXICAN CENTRAL Plateau. Roosters crow their morning wake-up call, and doves begin to coo from the rooftops. The first church bells peal the call to morning mass. Ready to begin a busy day, a few women step onto the sidewalk with buckets and brooms. They sweep and scrub until the pavement sparkles. The swish of brooms and clatter of buckets are among the sounds of early morning.

Down the street comes a boy banging a metal gong. Its clanging announces that the garbage truck is on its way. Doors burst open, and people step outside, hauling their bags of trash. They hand the bags up to the men on the truck, shouting an exchange of cheerful greetings.

Opposite: **Many houses in Mexico are painted bright colors.**

Going to School

Under Mexican law, all children must complete the ninth grade. Primary school, or *primaria*, goes from first through sixth grade. Secondary school, or *secundaria*, includes seventh, eighth, and ninth grades. Students who continue their education attend *preparatoria*. This four-year school prepares students to study for a profession. Students can go directly from preparatoria to medical school, law school, or teacher training.

Soon noisy bands of children set out for school. Mexican schoolchildren all wear uniforms. Classes tend to be large, with fifty students or more. The teachers expect students to be orderly and respectful.

Mexican Houses

In town, Mexican houses are built of brick or stone. Instead of having lawns and gardens outside, each house is built around a central patio or courtyard. The kitchen, living room, and dining room usually open off the patio. The roof is flat and can be reached by a stairway. Surrounded by a wall, the flat roof is part of the living area. It is common for a family to have a party on the roof.

Mexican children wear uniforms to school.

In rural areas and in poor sections of the towns and cities, houses are much simpler. There may be only one or two rooms and a tiny patio. The house may have a dirt floor and a roof made from sheets of tin. There is little furniture. At night straw mats called *petates* are unrolled. Everyone sleeps on the petates on the floor.

Many poor homes do not have electricity or running water. To get water for drinking and washing, people fill pails at a public tap. A kerosene-burning lantern provides light. People go to bed soon after dark and rise with the dawn.

Many houses in Mexico have patios, where people can sit outside and enjoy the pleasant weather.

Once the children are off to school, their mothers set out to do the day's shopping. They might go to a big new supermarket. Its shelves are lined with food in cans and boxes. Though supermarkets are popular, there is nothing like the open market for fresh fruits and vegetables. Some of the produce sold in the market is trucked in from faraway parts of the country, and some comes from nearby farms. The market offers a delicious array of fruits rarely seen in the United States and Canada. These include the pomegranate, its inside filled with edible seeds; the sweet, fibrous mango; the tangy guayaba; and the smooth and delicious mamey.

Tortillas are served with nearly every Mexican meal. Meat, vegetables, or eggs can be rolled up in a tortilla to create a

From Grinding Stone to Griddle

The making of tortillas is a long and complex process. After the kernels of corn are stripped from the cob they are soaked overnight in lime water and then ground into flour, or masa. Traditionally, women ground the masa using a cylindrical stone called a *mana*. The women rolled the mana over the corn kernels on a flat stone called a metate. It took many backbreaking hours to grind enough masa to make a day's worth of tortillas. Once the masa was ground, the cook shaped the wet dough into flat, round pancakes by patting it between her hands. For hundreds of years, the pat, pat, pat of a woman making tortillas was a familiar sound in Mexican households. Once shaped, the tortillas were grilled on a steaming griddle.

Today, most people in the towns buy their tortillas from a factory called a *tortillería*. Factory-made tortillas have made life far easier for Mexican women. But the squeal of the machine that churns out piping hot tortillas can never take the place of the homey pat, pat, pat that so many Mexicans fondly remember.

Mole Poblano

One of Mexico's most popular treats is a thick, rich sauce called *mole poblano*. It comes in many varieties, and each family tends to have its own cherished recipe. A good mole sauce generally has twenty or thirty ingredients, and some use as many as one hundred! The sauce may be made with several kinds of chili peppers, almonds, peanuts, sugar, cinnamon, cloves, and much more. One ingredient found in all mole recipes is bittersweet chocolate. The chocolate gives the sauce a unique flavor and a rich golden-brown color.

Mole originated in the city of Puebla during the sixteenth century. According to legend, nuns from the Convent of Santa Rosa learned that the archbishop was planning to visit. They had no idea what to serve him and prayed desperately for guidance. An angel appeared and gave them a recipe. Following the angel's instructions they chopped, stirred, and blended. They created a sauce that delighted the bishop and has been a favorite with millions of others.

taco. In rural areas people use tortillas instead of forks and spoons to scoop up rice, beans, or other foods.

The chili pepper is a basic ingredient in Mexican cooking. Chilis come in many varieties, some mild and some fiery hot. Chilis are usually served on the side, and a person can choose how spicy his or her food will be.

In general, Mexicans eat their main meal, or *comida*, in the middle of the day. In the past, stores and offices closed between two and four in the afternoon so that workers could

go home to eat with their families. This closing time is called the siesta, or rest period. People often found time for a nap after eating. Today, more and more workers commute to their jobs and do not have time to go home to eat. Businesses in towns and cities have begun to stay open all day long. The tradition of the leisurely siesta has faded away.

About 28 percent of the people in Mexico are under age fifteen.

Toys and Games

When school lets out, many children go home to help their families. Children often serve customers in family-run shops or wait on tables in family-operated restaurants. Older children are expected to help take care of their younger brothers and sisters. Because they are asked to help so much at home, Mexican children learn to be responsible at an early age.

Despite their responsibilities, Mexican children find time to play. Traditional toys include ceramic people and animals,

The Serpent of the Sea

At parties Mexican children sometimes play *la víbora de la mar* (the serpent of the sea), a game similar to London Bridge. Two players form an arch with their arms. The rest of the players make a line that snakes its way around the room, passing beneath the arch of hands. While walking, the children sing a song that begins, "*A la víbora, víbora de la mar, Todos quieren a pasar.*" ("By the serpent, serpent of the sea, Everybody wants to pass.") When the song ends, the player under the arch is out. The last player left is the winner.

rubber balls, marionettes, and tiny furniture and cooking utensils. Children often play soccer in a quiet street. They scramble out of the way when a car approaches and resume the game as soon as it passes by.

Children in Mexico play soccer anywhere there is open space.

Fiesta Time

Weddings and saints' days are special occasions that bring people together to celebrate. Besides these personal celebrations, Mexicans enjoy religious and patriotic holidays throughout the year. Whatever the holiday may be, there is a procession. Schoolchildren usually march and sing.

Calendar of Holidays

Three Kings Day	January 6
Carnival	February–March
Good Friday	March–April
Easter Sunday	March–April
Cinco de Mayo	May 5
St. John's Day	June 24
Corpus Christi	June–July
Independence Day	September 16
St. Michael's Day	September 29
Day of the Dead	November 1
Day of Our Lady of Guadalupe	December 12
Days of the Christmas celebration	December 16–25

One of the most joyous holidays is Carnival, a time of music and feasting. The biggest Carnival celebrations take place in Mazatlán and Veracruz and draw visitors from around the world. Carnival usually begins with the Burning of Ill Humor, the burning of a figure dressed to look like an unpopular political leader. There follows a week of dancing and games

¡Pas!

In many towns it is a Carnival custom for children to buy colored eggshells stuffed with confetti. Eggs in hand, the children sneak up on unwary partygoers. A child cries, "¡Pas!" ("Pow!") as she or he cracks an egg over someone's head, releasing a blizzard of confetti.

and the crowning of a king and queen. Carnival ends when Lent begins. Lent is a forty-day period before Easter, when devout people give up pleasures.

Carnival is a joyous time, filled with costumes and parades.

On September 15, the evening before Independence Day, the president of Mexico delivers the Grito de Independencia (Shout of Independence). Five times during the president's six-year term, he or she gives the Grito in front of the National Palace in Mexico City. The president delivers the Grito in Dolores Hidalgo during his or her last year in office. The Grito is a reenactment of Father Hidalgo's call to arms that launched the War of Independence in 1810. "Long live

Felipe Calderón gives the traditional Grito to kick off the independence day celebrations in 2009.

independence!" the president shouts to the crowd. "Long live our heroes! Long live Mexico!" At the final shout, the crowd goes wild with cheers and applause. Bands burst into song, and fireworks displays shower the scene with dazzling colors.

One of Mexico's most fascinating holidays is the Day of the Dead, celebrated on November 1. Families remember their departed friends and relatives by setting up altars in their honor. The altar may be decorated with photos, poems, and treasured objects. Later, families gather in the cemetery at the graves of their loved ones. They bring the loved one's favorite foods, which they place upon the grave. The visit to the cemetery is not a time of sadness. It is a celebration and a renewal of loving ties with those who are gone.

During the Christmas season Mexicans re-create Mary and Joseph's journey to Bethlehem before the birth of the Christ child. For ten nights before Christmas, families host *posadas*, or Christmas parties. The word *posada* means "inn." When guests arrive to join a posada celebration, they knock on the door and ask, "Is there room at the inn tonight?"

During Day of the Dead celebrations, people sometimes dress up as skeletons.

La Pastorela

A Christmas tradition in some Mexican towns is the performance of a *pastorela*. The pastorela is a pageant that tells the Christmas story in music and verse. Townspeople of all ages take part, dressing as shepherds, wise men, innkeepers, soldiers, and members of the Holy Family. The pastorela has its roots in sixteenth-century Spain. It has evolved endlessly over the centuries. Today's pastorelas may include clowns, magicians, policemen, politicians, and many more characters who were never part of the original story.

Mexican children traditionally did not receive presents on Christmas Day. The day for exchanging gifts was Three Kings Day, January 6. Three Kings Day celebrates the day when the three wise men are supposed to have reached Bethlehem with gifts for the Christ child. More and more, Mexican families now celebrate Christmas with the giving of presents.

A Walk Through the Plaza

As the day draws to a close, people gather in the plaza at the center of town. Children dart back and forth playing tag or hide-and-seek. Their parents sit on benches and chat with their neighbors. Vendors sell balloons, wind-up toys, and fruit-flavored ices. Birds chatter sleepily in the treetops. Church bells announce the evening mass.

Suddenly a mariachi band breaks into song. The band is playing one of Mexico's most beloved melodies, "Cielito Lindo." ("Pretty Little Sky.") Some of the people on the benches join in the refrain. Their voices mingle with the bells as they sing, "¡Ay, ay, ay, ay! ¡Canta y no llores!" ("Sing and don't cry!")

Mexico has endured cruel wars and vicious dictators. Its people have survived droughts and earthquakes, and they face an uncertain future. Whatever comes their way, Mexicans keep on singing.

Men selling balloons are a common sight in town plazas.

Timeline

Mexico History

The first humans enter Mexico.	**ca. 13,000** BCE
Humans begin to plant maize in Mexico's Central Valley.	**5000** BCE
Maya culture reaches its high point.	200–800 CE
According to Aztec legend, the wandering tribe sees an eagle on a cactus and founds Tenochtitlán.	1325
Hernán Cortés lands an expedition in the Gulf Coast of Mexico and marches to Tenochtitlán.	1519
The Spaniards conquer the Aztecs and establish the colony of New Spain.	1521
An indigenous farmer named Juan Diego sees the miraculous vision of Our Lady of Guadalupe.	1531
Father Miguel Hidalgo begins to call for Mexico's independence from Spain.	1810
Mexico becomes an independent nation.	1821
Santa Anna crushes Texas rebels at the Battle of the Alamo.	1836

World History

ca. 2500 BCE	Egyptians build the pyramids and the Sphinx in Giza.
ca. 563 BCE	The Buddha is born in India.
313 CE	The Roman emperor Constantine legalizes Christianity.
610	The Prophet Muhammad begins preaching a new religion called Islam.
1054	The Eastern (Orthodox) and Western (Roman Catholic) Churches break apart.
1095	The Crusades begin.
1215	King John seals the Magna Carta.
1300s	The Renaissance begins in Italy.
1347	The plague sweeps through Europe.
1453	Ottoman Turks capture Constantinople, conquering the Byzantine Empire.
1492	Columbus arrives in North America.
1500s	Reformers break away from the Catholic Church, and Protestantism is born.
1776	The U.S. Declaration of Independence is signed.
1789	The French Revolution begins.

Mexico History

Mexico is defeated in the U.S.-Mexican War, losing all of its territory north of the Rio Grande.	1848
Maximilian I is executed after France tries to establish Mexico as a colony.	1867
Francisco Madero is elected president, triggering the Mexican Revolution of 1910.	1910
A constitutional congress meets in Querétaro and writes a constitution granting many new rights to the people.	1917
The Cristero War breaks out.	1927
Lázaro Cárdenas is elected president and launches a series of reforms.	1934
Mexican women win the right to vote.	1953
Mexico City hosts the Olympic Games.	1968
Octavio Paz becomes the first Mexican to win the Nobel Prize in Literature.	1990
A group, mostly Indians, called the Zapatistas launches a rebellion in Chiapas.	1994
Vicente Fox is elected president, breaking the hold of the Institutional Revolutionary Party.	2000
Mexico celebrates the bicentennial of the War of Independence and the hundredth anniversary of the Mexican Revolution.	2010

World History

1865	The American Civil War ends.
1879	The first practical lightbulb is invented.
1914	World War I begins.
1917	The Bolshevik Revolution brings communism to Russia.
1929	A worldwide economic depression begins.
1939	World War II begins.
1945	World War II ends.
1957	The Vietnam War begins.
1969	Humans land on the Moon.
1975	The Vietnam War ends.
1989	The Berlin Wall is torn down as communism crumbles in Eastern Europe.
1991	The Soviet Union breaks into separate states.
2001	Terrorists attack the World Trade Center in New York City and the Pentagon in Washington, D.C.
2004	A tsunami in the Indian Ocean destroys coastlines in Africa, India, and Southeast Asia.
2008	The United States elects its first African American president.

Fast Facts

Official name: Estados Unidos Mexicanos
(United Mexican States)

Capital: Mexico City

Official language: Spanish

Teotihuacán

Mexican flag

Mountains

Official religion:	None
National anthem:	"Himno Nacional de México" (National Anthem of Mexico)
Government:	Federal republic
Chief of state and head of government:	President
Area:	758,449 square miles (1,964,374 sq km)
Bordering countries:	United States to the north; Guatemala and Belize to the south
Arable land:	12.66% of the land is suitable for farming
Highest elevation:	Pico de Orizaba, 18,410 feet (5,611 m) above sea level
Lowest elevation:	Mexicali Valley, 33 feet (10 m) below sea level
Longest river:	Rio Grande, which Mexico shares with the United States, 1,248 miles (2,008 km) within Mexico
Longest river entirely within Mexico:	Río Lerma, about 350 miles (560 km)
Largest lake:	Lake Chapala, 417 square miles (1,080 sq km)
Length of coastlines:	5,797 miles (9,329 km)
Average Annual Precipitation:	Mexico City, 30 inches (76 cm)

National Cathedral

Currency

National population (2010 est.): 113,724,226

Population of largest cities (2009 est.):
Mexico City: 12,294,193
Ecatepec: 1,806,226
Guadalajara: 1,640,589
Puebla: 1,590,256
Ciudad Juárez: 1,512,354

Famous landmarks:
▶ *Guadalajara Cathedral,* Guadalajara
▶ *National Cathedral,* Mexico City
▶ *National Museum of Anthropology and History,* Mexico City
▶ *Teatro Juárez,* Guanajuato
▶ *Teotihuacán,* Mexico City

Economy: Tourism is one of the most important parts of the nation's economy. Although it varies from year to year, about four million Mexicans are employed in the tourist industry. Oil production is another important part of the economy. Mexico is the seventh-largest producer of oil in the world. Mexican factories churn out processed foods, chemical products, iron and steel, and automobiles. Among the most important crops grown in Mexico are corn, wheat, rice, beans, and cotton.

Currency: The peso. In May 2011, 11.7 pesos equaled one U.S. dollar.

System of weights and measures: Metric system

Literacy rate: 92.8%

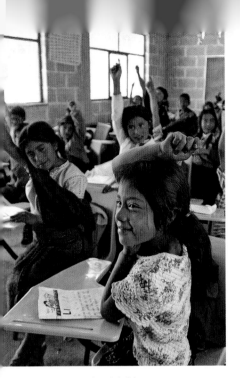

Schoolchildren

Emiliano Zapata

Common Spanish words and phrases:		
	Adiós	good-bye
	hola	hello
	por favor	please
	gracias	thank you
	¿Cómo está usted?	How are you?
	¿Qué hora es?	What time is it?
	¿Cómo te llamas?	What is your name?

Prominent Mexicans:		
	Plácido Domingo *Opera singer*	(1941–)
	Benito Juárez *President*	(1806–1872)
	Frida Kahlo *Artist*	(1907–1954)
	Octavio Paz *Nobel Prize–winning writer*	(1914–1998)
	Diego Rivera *Painter*	(1886–1957)
	Carlos Slim Helú *Businessperson*	(1940–)
	Pancho Villa *Revolutionary*	(1878–1923)
	Emiliano Zapata *Revolutionary leader*	(ca.1879–1919)

To Find Out More

Books

▶ Gelletly, LeeAnne. *Mexican Immigration*. Philadelphia: Mason Crest Publishers, 2004.

▶ Harris, Nathaniel. *Ancient Maya: Archaeology Unlocks the Secrets of the Maya's Past*. Washington, DC: National Geographic, 2008.

▶ Johnston, Tony. *The Ancestors Are Singing*. New York: Farrar Straus Giroux, 2003.

▶ Kalman, Bobbie. *Mexico: The Culture*. New York: Crabtree, 2009.

▶ MacMillan, Dianne. *Mexican Independence Day and Cinco de Mayo*. Berkeley Heights, NJ: Enslow, 2008.

▶ Serrano, Francisco. *The Poet King of Tezcoco: A Great Leader of Ancient Mexico*. Toronto, ON and Berkeley, CA: House of Anansi, 2007.

▶ Stein, R. Conrad. *The Story of Mexico: Cortés and the Spanish Conquest*. Greensboro, NC: Morgan Reynolds, 2008.

DVDs

▶ *Ancient Maya*. Wynnewood, PA: Schlessinger Media, 2004.

▶ *Cinco de Mayo*. Wynnewood, PA: Schlessinger Media, 2004.

▶ *Mexico*. Wynnewood, PA: Schlessinger Media, 2005.

▶ *Revolutionary Mexico: 1910–1940*. Wynnewood, PA: Schlessinger Media, 2005.

Web Sites

▶ **Countries and Their Cultures**
www.everyculture.com/Ma-Ni
/Mexico.html
*For information about food, customs,
family life, history, arts and crafts,
and more.*

▶ **History.com: Mexico**
www.history.com/topics/mexico
*For an overview of Mexican
history and links to many articles
and a detailed timeline.*

▶ **Indigenous Peoples of Mexico**
www.indigenouspeople.net/mex
_main.htm
*To find articles, photos, and music
relating to all of the indigenous peoples of Mexico, past and present.*

▶ **Mexconnect**
www.mexconnect.com
/articles/3148-mexico-history
-time-line-overview-resource-page
*Offers a timeline of Mexican history
with links to maps, pictures, and
dozens of related articles.*

Embassies

▶ **Embassy of Mexico**
1911 Pennsylvania Avenue
Washington, DC 20006
202/728-1600
http://embamex.sre.gob.mx/usa

▶ **Embassy of Mexico in Canada**
45 O'Connor St., Suite 1000
Ottawa, Ontario K1P 1A4
613/233-8988
http://embamex.sre.gob.mx
/canada_eng

Index

Page numbers in *italics*
indicate illustrations.

Meet the Author

I GREW UP IN LITTLE FALLS, New Jersey, where I was the first blind student to attend the local public school. I graduated from Oberlin College and earned a master's degree from Smith College School for Social Work. After working for several years at University Settlement House in New York, I moved to the town of San Miguel de Allende in central Mexico. In San Miguel I wrote my first book, a young-adult novel called *Belonging* (Dial Press, 1978). In San Miguel, I also helped start the Centro de Crecimiento (Center for Growing), a school for children with disabilities. Today, I live in Chicago with my husband, children's writer R. Conrad (Dick) Stein; we have one daughter, Janna. We visit Mexico as often as we can. It is our home away from home.

I have written nearly two dozen young-adult novels and numerous nonfiction titles for young readers. My most

recent fiction is the Saddle the Wind series (Kingfisher, 2006), four historical novels about girls and horses. Among my nonfiction titles are *Witchcraft Trials: Fear, Betrayal, and Death in Salem* (Enslow, 2009); *Snake Pits, Talking Cures, and Magic Bullets: A History of Mental Illness* (Millbrook, 2003); and many titles in the America the Beautiful series published by Scholastic.

In writing this book about Mexico, I drew upon my rich trove of memories from the years I lived there full-time and my countless shorter visits. Any time I needed to verify a fact or get a second opinion about an impression, I turned to my enthusiastic network of San Miguel friends. I wish to extend special thanks to Liliana Zúñiga for graciously sharing her story of undocumented immigration.

I also explored some wonderful literature about Mexico, books written by foreign travelers and those written by Mexicans themselves. *Mexican Days*, by Tony Cohan; *Mexico in Mind*, edited by Maria Finn; and *The Labyrinth of Solitude*, by Octavio Paz evoked a sense of place and showed me again the spirit of the Mexican people. I discovered a nearly forgotten gem in *A Treasury of Mexican Folkways* by Frances Toor. First published in 1947, it describes a land that has undergone dramatic changes, but many of the customs that Toor witnessed are still very much alive today.

Photo Credits